Tough on Hate?

CRITICAL ISSUES IN CRIME AND SOCIETY
Raymond J. Michalowski, Series Editor

Critical Issues in Crime and Society is oriented toward critical analysis of contemporary problems in crime and justice. The series is open to a broad range of topics including specific types of crime, wrongful behavior by economically or politically powerful actors, controversies over justice system practices, and issues related to the intersection of identity, crime, and justice. It is committed to offering thoughtful works that will be accessible to scholars and professional criminologists, general readers, and students.

For a list of titles in the series, see the last page of the book.

Tough on Hate?

THE CULTURAL POLITICS OF HATE CRIMES

CLARA S. LEWIS

RUTGERS UNIVERSITY PRESS
New Brunswick, New Jersey, and London

LIBRARY OF CONGRESS CATALOGING-IN-PUBLICATION DATA

Lewis, Clara S., 1981–
    Tough on hate? : the cultural politics of hate crimes / Clara S. Lewis.pages cm. —
(Critical issues in crime and society)
    Includes bibliographical references and index.
    ISBN 978–0–8135–6231–5 (hardcover : alk. paper) — ISBN 978–0–8135–6230–8
(pbk. : alk. paper) — ISBN 978–0–8135–6232–2 (e-book)
    1. Hate crimes—United States. I. Title.
    KF9345.L49 2013
    364.150973—dc23
      2013010367

A British Cataloging-in-Publication record for this book
is available from the British Library.

"Charlie Howard's Descent," from Turtle Swan by Mark Doty, reprinted by permission
of David R. Godine, Publisher, Inc. Copyright © 1987 by Mark Doty.

Visit our website: http://rutgerspress.rutgers.edu

Manufactured in the United States of America

To the Essence of Non-Judgment, Mary Lewis,
And her namesake, Marsden

Contents

ACKNOWLEDGMENTS

THE IDEAS THAT SHAPE this book have evolved in conversation with many wonderful, thoughtful people. Among the scholars who have informed the direction of this book, I am particularly indebted to professors from George Washington University's American studies and sociology departments, namely Thomas Guglielmo, William Chambliss, Ivy Leigh Ken, Melani McAlister, and Joseph Kip Kosek, and Smith College's sociology department and American studies program, namely Ginetta Candelario, Daniel Horowitz, Marc Steinberg, and Myron Peretz Glazer. Guglielmo's critical insight, generous comments, balanced attitude, and personal warmth were an invaluable resource. At GWU, I was also fortunate to be part of a graduate student writing group whose members, Charity Fox, Joan Fragaszy Troyano, Jeannine Love, Jennifer Cho, and Anne Showalter, provided unflagging support. My multiyear collaboration with these women has been one of the most nourishing homes my intellectual life has ever resided in. At Rutgers University Press, I have had the unmatched good fortune of working with Peter Mickulas and Raymond J. Michalowski Jr. In the final drafting stages, Sophie Hagen, beloved cousin and gifted editor, provided expert corrections and posed important questions about the project's implications.

In conducting research for this project, I received the assistance of a number of librarians and archivists. Cynthia Rufo from the Northeastern University Libraries Archives and Specials Collections Department, Malea Young from the Library of Congress's Newspaper and Current Periodical Reading Room, Matthew E. Braun from the Law Library of Congress, and Janet Olson from the George Washington University's Gelman Library each made crucial contributions.

Finally, I am delighted to have the opportunity to thank my family. My parents, Wendy Seligman Lewis and Paul Lewis, and two new arrivals, my husband, Casey Sussman, and my son, Marsden Lewis Sussman, are a source of perpetual inspiration. My life is charmed by the love we share.

Tough on Hate?

Chapter 1

Introduction

The Cultural Politics of Hate Crimes

> At the forefront of our minds, the obvious signals
> of violence are acts of crime and terror, civil unrest,
> international conflict. But we should learn to step back
> to disentangle ourselves from the fascinating lure of this
> directly visible "subjective" violence, violence performed
> by a clearly visible agent. We need to perceive the contours
> of the background which generate such outbursts. A step
> back enables us to identify a violence that sustains our
> very efforts to fight violence and to promote tolerance.
>
> —Slavoj Žižek, *Violence*

IT IS TEMPTING TO begin a book on hate crimes with violence. The words themselves, "hate" and "crime," evoke images of the most heinous acts of prejudicial assault. Within the U.S. mainstream cultural imagination, sadism, Nazism, and white power dramatize hate crimes stories. In considering the problem, we are invited to recall the same select few victims' degraded bodies. We see Matthew Shepard, Christlike, through the dark Wyoming night. His frail form strung up against a cattle fence, the tracks of his tears cutting lines down his bloodstained face. We see James Byrd Jr.'s dentures, thrown from his decapitated head into a drainage ditch, the rest of his torso reduced to smears across a three-mile stretch of backcountry Texas road. Our collective memory preserves the physical reality of these victims' suffering as evidence of bigotry's evil.

The most "obvious signals" of hate crimes remain the swastika, the Klansman's noose, and the skinhead's buzzed skull. These potent symbols have come to satisfy our expectation of what constitutes a hate crime. But the expectation itself as well as the images that sate it are misleading. If we have internalized a particular image of hate crimes, that image is itself the end result of historically specific work on the part of cultural producers, national political figures, and, to a lesser extent, advocates and academics. As theorist Slavoj Žižek, quoted in the epigraph, insists, a step back is necessary.

My first personal encounter with a hate crime lacked what Žižek describes as a "clearly visible agent." Indeed, the persistent absence of any kind of accountable criminal subject made the incident all the more hauntingly nasty. As with the majority of all hate crimes committed in the United States, the crime itself was a simple act of graffiti.[1] *Die Dyke, Die!* Scripted with matter-of-fact tidiness on a first-year student's dry erase board, the threat surfaced like a withering, long-suppressed resentment. Its unexpectedness unhinged us. The victim and I lived in the same undergraduate residence hall at Smith College. Located in western Massachusetts, Smith is one of the country's oldest women's colleges. Where many of its contemporaries went coeducational, Smith maintained its commitment to single-sex higher education. The resonance of this particular hate crime becomes comprehensible only if understood as located within Smith's distinct social milieu. As with hate crimes generally, both context and subtext matter.

A micro-universe of homosociability, Smith places students within a dormitory system that engenders a remarkable degree of trust and togetherness. Tellingly, students refer to their dorms as "houses." During the four years I lived on campus in Gardiner House, every meal was eaten with the same group of women, at the same table. It was prepared by the same staff, with the same radio station's outdated hits persistently humming behind the kitchen's routinized clunk and clatter. On a typical Monday, we might sulk home from class with that one absurdly difficult question from the morning's pop quiz trailing us, buzzard-like in its seeming doom and persistence, to be greeted by giant platters of grilled cheese sandwiches so deliciously greasy and well-salted that their browned crusts clearly shared genetic material with the French fry family; tart, steaming bowls of tomato soup; and Tom Petty's "Free Falling." Every other meal, ritual, and detail of the campus environment conspired to offer similar assurances of nurturance and academic motivation.

Throughout the year, the women in my house held hands, wore ugly hats, sang songs of dorm loyalty, and skinny-dipped. On more than one occasion, women who had previously defined themselves as straight would find something newly erotic about a close female friend and the terms of sexual self-identification would slide toward passionate renaming. BDOC: Big Dyke On Campus. LUG: Lesbian Until Graduation. These were terms of endearment and known categories within Smith's distinct sexual typology. Homosexual sex was in some (arguably confined) ways pervasive on Smith's campus. Acceptance of lesbian desire was presupposed, if not lavishly indulged.

We held dear a mythology about ourselves as a progressive community. Having transcended mere tolerance, we liked to tell ourselves that we had created an idealized diverse space. "Problematic" was our favorite buzzword; we used it to describe everything off campus. But the unique challenges of being a lesbian, or being queer, or being transgendered, or being a person of color, still affected the lives of many students, especially those who were not simply engaged in playful experimentation. Given this often overlooked tension, the slur *Die Dyke, Die!* cut through our imagined veil of tolerance and drew to the surface a more complex entanglement of sexual identities and hierarchies of sexual belonging. Ultimately, the progressive myths themselves intensified the harm caused by the crime.

The student who received the threat had been gay before arriving at Smith. Once on campus, he stopped using female pronouns, adopted a male name, and began the process of transitioning from female to male. He was husky and butch and had tried drugs I had heard about only during DARE lectures. "Dyke" was hardly how he defined himself. Even before the hate crime crystallized his marginality, the other feminine first-year students already held him at a distance.

The night after the graffiti was discovered, I found myself sitting on the fourth floor hallway with a cluster of overwhelmed first-year students who were trying, awkwardly, to make sense of the incident. This was my first exposure to the defensive rhetoric that follows in the wake of a publicly recognized hate crime—the overwhelming desire to prove that *we*, the people within the community where the crime occurred, are better than the crime. These women were embarrassed by the crime and felt that the house's reputation had been unfairly tarnished: *This is not us. This makes us look bad. It isn't fair that this makes us look bad. Why is this happening to us? Maybe he wrote it himself to get attention.* On one superficial level, they were right. Before the hate crime, we had a stellar campus-wide reputation for throwing fun, theme-based keg parties (our vampire luau was a yearly favorite). The crime made our house an object of muted disdain on campus and an unfortunate playground for new Residence Life diversity initiatives.

Intense as they were at the time, our feelings of shame, embarrassment, and indignation compromised our ability to support the victim, who was appalled by our fuss over the dorm's public image. As the victim stopped attending meals in our dining room, we focused our collective energies on demanding that the institution ramp up its efforts to identify the crime's perpetrator. Firmly believing that finding the culprit would solve the problem, we insisted that the administration come and take all of our fingerprints and do a thorough crime scene investigation. Never mind that the logistics of writing on a dry erase board made such a demand for justice nearly impossible for campus authorities to satisfy.

In retrospect, I understand that by the time we were actively investigating the crime the nature of the problem had already shifted. The crime itself was actionably serious, harmful, and wrong. Beyond being a minor property violation, it had profound social and psychological consequences. If a perpetrator had been identified, he or she should have been punished fully in accord with the heightened seriousness of the offense's bias motivation. However, by the time we were all eagerly demanding retribution for the initial incident, the victim himself had moved on to dealing with the isolation and betrayal that accompanied the dorm's defensive response. Our response created a new set of problems. In defending our dorm's reputation we had further marginalized the crime's actual victim. He moved out of our dorm the following year. The perpetrator was never identified.

In many ways, this book is an effort to productively engage the memory of this incident. I aim to articulate a fuller understanding of the social harm caused, not by hate crimes themselves, but by the ideological premises that shape how we respond to hate crimes. Hate crimes are a distinct category of criminal violation that call for rigorous, informed policing and fair adjudication. This analysis encounters hate crimes not primarily as criminal incidents, however, but as a universe of densely packed ideas about difference, about what constitutes harm, and about whose trauma is worthy of resources, recognition, and respect. I insist that certain mainstream ideas about hate crimes are part of the problem and that effective anti-hate-crime efforts require not only, or even predominantly, law enforcement remedies but also an engagement with deeply held cultural and political values.

Unfortunately, hate crimes tend to be represented in ways that not only dismiss these important underlying values but also favor gory crime scene details over the nuances of local history, context, and community. This is particularly troubling because it means that the holistic perspective of civil and minority rights advocates—who argue that hate crimes need to be countered within a broad effort to promote social justice—gets drowned out. In detailing this dynamic, *Tough on Hate?* demonstrates that narratives about hate crimes contain a sharp irony: the sympathetic attention we pay to certain shocking hate crime murders further legitimizes an already pervasive unwillingness to act on the urgent civil rights issues of our time. Worse still, it reveals the widespread acceptance of ideas about difference, tolerance, and crime that work against future progress on behalf of historically marginalized communities

UNDERSTANDING HATE CRIMES IN A "POST-DIFFERENCE" SOCIETY

On a national scale, political speech and cultural production inform our sense of what hate crimes are. The news media and national politicians frame the issue for their audiences: news consumers and voters. In doing so, they suggest what kinds of actions constitute hate crimes and how citizens should respond to these incidents. These empowered social actors' varied investments in defining the hate crime problem, as a signal to voters from historically marginalized groups, as a stance against crime, and as an attention-worthy news theme, are fundamentally at stake in this inquiry.

How the mainstream news media, national politicians, federal lawmakers, law enforcement authorities, advocates, and academics all subtly manage the meaning of hate crimes through framing practices and definitional contests is, in and of itself, a fraught political process that has changed significantly over time. What are the epistemological foundations of hate crimes in the United States? How has the issue been represented to the public? What does a close reading of the framing of hate crimes in the political sphere and news media reveal about the values and norms of our society?

From the mid-1990s up until the election of President Barack Obama in 2008, the most widely distributed depictions of hate crimes shared thematic features, followed similar narrative trajectories, and were populated by familiar criminological figures. During this period, the hate crimes that garnered sustained national attention tended to be hyper-violent murders committed by clearly guilty perpetrators who belonged to white power groups. As these stories unfolded on the national stage, audiences were invited to memorize graphic crime scene details, pity the families of innocent victims, and follow courtroom dramas that ended cleanly with harsh convictions. A death sentence often proffered the most satisfying conclusion to these elaborate rituals of crime and punishment.

The most evident observation is that these narratives narrowly defined bigotry as both extremist criminal activity and a law enforcement problem. Counterintuitively, these narratives also celebrated American exceptionalism; perpetuated stereotypes about mental illness, criminality, and masculinity; further marginalized the white underclass; elevated romanticized images of passive victims; promoted defenses of color blindness; and insisted that prejudice was part of a transcended history. Speaking out against hate crimes opened opportunities for journalists, broadcasters, and politicians to demonize white supremacists, while also limiting the relevance of contemporary civil rights struggles. In sum, representations of hate crimes both depoliticized and decontextualized the problem.

Put into a broader historical framework, these narratives echo the problematic racial politics that characterized prominent civil rights era visual media. In his recent analysis of civil rights era photography, cultural historian Martin Berger demonstrates that iconic photographs of the civil rights movement, such as the infamous images of Birmingham's police dogs and fire hoses, tapped into liberal white sympathy by casting black activists in the role of passive victims of irrational southern white violence. These images nudged liberal whites toward supporting the era's important legislative reforms. But the prominence of these rallying images both erased the legacy of active black resistance and undermined the potential for more sweeping, radical social change.[2] Hate crimes inherit, re-entrench, and perpetuate this difficult legacy's conceptual apparatus, or its ideas about racism and antiracism. The very concept of hate crime, which has frequently been described with stultifying optimism as the "final" frontier in the battle for civil rights, is in large part premised on an acceptance of these earlier images' core idea that racism is characterized by the obvious force of physical violence. The journalistic and political fascination with hate crimes that began in the late 1980s can even be seen as the next logical step beyond popular images of the African American civil rights movement: within this period's frenzied attentiveness to hate crime murders, moderate white audiences were again treated to representations of bigotry that clearly did not implicate them, that provoked limited legislative reforms, and that misrepresented the nature of the vulnerability experienced by people of color and homosexuals. Like their civil rights era precursors, depictions of hate crimes tend to exclude images of potentially threatening agency on the part of nonwhite and homosexual actors.

The problems this kind of cultural work poses to antiracism have been well documented. What my examination of hate crimes freshly reveals is that the enforcement of color-blind racism and postracialism now challenges efforts to combat not only racism, but also homophobia, xenophobia, and anti-Arab and Muslim sentiment. Color-blind racism is the widely held belief among whites that it is best for Americans individually to act as if they are incapable of seeing racial difference and collectively to reject state policies that proactively seek to remedy histories of racial inequality, most significantly affirmative action. Closely related to color-blind racism, postracialism is the assumption that we are currently living in a "postracial" nation, meaning that race and racism are no longer salient features of American life. The myth of the postracial nation is the direct result of prioritizing color blindness. If color blindness is the aspiration, postracialism is the prize. Despite the many partisan divisions of our current political climate, these two ideas about race are widely accepted on both sides of the aisle. Even President Obama's first major speech directly addressing race, "A More Perfect Union," lent credence to these false suppositions.[3]

Like numerous other contemporary cultural products, mainstream depictions of hate crimes provide evidence that color-blind racism and postracialism no longer reside solely in discussions about race; these theories have migrated into entirely different debates over the political rights and social status of sexual, religious, and ethnic minority groups. To describe this seepage, or perhaps more accurately repurposing, I develop a new theoretical construct: "post-difference ideology." Post-difference ideology describes the phenomenon whereby the thought processes, or ideological patterns, that sustain color-blind racism have come to characterize not only racial thinking but approaches to understanding other forms of difference and bias as well. This post-difference ideology is evident when victims of anti-Arab or anti-Muslim violence praise American society. It appears when victims of homophobic violence are introduced to national news viewers through outdated images from their childhoods, gaining sympathy by mere association with the tropes of heterosexual family life. Post-difference ideology can be seen doing the subtle, associative work of offsetting guilt, limiting culpability, and thwarting broader recognition of minority grievances. Dishearteningly for those invested in social and racial justice, this cultural work takes place under the guise of what is popularly understood as "combating" hate crimes or getting "tough" on hate. It is important to note that numerous other studies document the pervasive quality of both color-blind racism and postracialism. However, it is still surprising to find evidence of these deeply demobilizing views used in explanations of hate crimes, one of the very few culturally visible and politically accessible means of recognizing bias.

While post-difference ideology has come to characterize mainstream depictions of hate crimes and now saturates political speech dedicated to the problem, it flies in the face of what social scientists, psychologists, criminologists, and, more recently, geographers have discovered. With near uniformity, empirically grounded academic analyses of hate crimes focus attention on the way in which these offenses express the multitude of biases, prejudices, and stereotypes that define our shared social life. Scholars of the subject with very different disciplinary and political backgrounds agree that hate crimes are nested social events.[4] Each hate crime reflects a specific community's history, values, and ongoing struggles. As the American Psychological Association concluded in 1998, the vast majority of hate crimes perpetrators "do not fit the stereotype of the hate-filled extremist." Instead, "they are average young people who often do not see anything wrong with their behavior."[5] Despite the robust quality of research on hate crimes' social foundations, the narratives about hate crimes that garner national attention and solicit presidential rebuke uniformly revolve around stories of individual murder victims, the monsters who killed them, and the exceptional nation that adjudicates retributive justice. Post-difference ideology is the background against which these spectacularly brutal crime stories make sense as antibias speech and within which social critique becomes seemingly irrelevant.

Anti-hate-crime legislation, when implemented properly at the local level, functions as a sound criminal justice practice.[6] However, mainstream images of and narratives about hate crimes share the same damning consequences for members of historically marginalized groups as other expressions of color blindness. Within these representations, bigotry is unequivocally defined as criminal, which demonstrates progress beyond the U.S. history of legally mandated segregation and discrimination. But the intergroup differences that initiated these crimes in the first place are rendered meaningless beyond the limited confines of the individual criminal's deranged mind; structural and identity-based differences, such as race, ethnicity, sexual orientation, and religion, are viewed as meaningful only to a lunatic, criminal fringe. These representations simultaneously reinforce the idea that bigotry is deviant, while also implicitly suggesting that belonging to a historically marginalized group is irrelevant. The myth of the color-blind society transmogrifies within these narratives into the myth of the post-difference society.

ETYMOLOGY

The concept of hate crimes is a historically specific cultural, political, and legal invention of the post–civil rights era. While prominent hate crimes stories from the 1990s have achieved a macabre familiarity, the limited nature of the concept's cultural and political scope was not inevitable. Nor were the now standard associations that conflate hate crimes with hate group activity and murders predetermined. Instead, the intimate relationship hate crimes now share with post-difference ideology goes against the very interests of the parties who initially identified the problem and sought to remedy it. By tracing the etymology of the phrase from the 1960s to the 1990s, we can illuminate how it has been both depoliticized and embedded within the "war on crime."

The exact etymology of the phrase "hate crimes" remains more elusive than previous authors admit.[7] Scholars have credited both the Anti-Defamation League's (ADL) 1981 model statute and the Hate Crime Statistics Act (HCSA) of 1985 with coining the phrase.[8] As prior etymologies state, the first use of the term "hate crimes" in the *Congressional Record* appeared when Congressman Mario Biaggi (D, NY) introduced the HCSA on July 22, 1985. However, early uses of the term in the print news media as well as internal documents from the ADL, the Boston Police Department's Community Disorders Unit (CDU), and other minority rights groups working on issues of bias-motivated victimization during the 1980s reveal more complexity in the term's origin and evolution.

The *Oxford English Dictionary* (OED) did not add the term "hate crimes" until June 2002. The dictionary's current entry on hate crimes, which falls as a subheading under the word "hate," suggests that the phrase originated in the United States and cites a July 14, 1984, *Washington Post* article as the first example of usage.[9] However, the OED fails to note that the *Washington Post* article was preceded by two other articles. The term appears to have first been published in the *Chicago Daily Defender*. On April 5, 1960, the *Defender* printed an article titled "Urges Law on Hate Crimes" that reported on Governor Gaylord Nelson's (D, WI) effort to make "lynching" and "hate bombings" federal crimes.[10] Over twenty years later, on January 11, 1984, the *Baltimore Sun* published an article titled "Divided Council Approves Penalties for Racist Attacks" that included the next print appearance of the term. As this brief history reveals, the phrase "hate crimes" first appeared in a historically African American newspaper to describe white-on-black violence during the civil rights era and was simply ignored by other sources at the time.

The term "hate crimes" resurfaced more prominently in the mid-1980s. After the *Washington Post*'s 1984 article, the next news source to print the phrase "hate crimes" was the *Christian Science Monitor*, on December 23, 1986. The third source—the *New York Times*—did not print the phrase until March 2, 1987.[11] Television news networks did not begin using it until even later. CBS News and ABC News reported their first hate crimes stories in 1990, and NBC did not use the term until 1997.

Although the phrase "hate crimes" eventually became a media favorite, it was initially employed exclusively by law enforcement authorities and state legislators. During the 1980s and early 1990s, the term appeared in articles that quoted law enforcement officials or that reported on proposed state-level anti-hate-crime laws. For example, in the 1986 *Christian Science Monitor* article cited above, the phrase "hate crimes" was included within a direct quotation from New York City Police Commissioner Benjamin Ward, who stated, "It was a bias incident, a hate crime."[12] Similarly, in the 1984 *Washington Post* article cited above, the phrase "hate crimes" was buried within a report on a speech Boston Mayor Flynn gave to the law enforcement community on policing practices. As these examples illustrate, the term "hate crimes" only haltingly entered into popular usage during several years of dialogue among law enforcement officials, legislators, and the print news media. However, the media were notably skeptical in their initial adoption of the term—in describing the new legislation and reporting on local interethnic urban conflicts, the *New York Times* used the phrase "so-called hate crimes" as late as 1991.[13]

Despite early echoes, the phrase "hate crimes" was not politicized, popularized, and codified into law until the late 1980s and the early 1990s when tough-on-crime politics were in full bloom. During this period of intense criminal justice reform, the terms used to label the phenomenon of bias-motivated victimization in the United States changed radically. The news media and politicians collected offenses that were originally labeled "community disorders," "civil rights violations," "racially motivated attacks," "gay bashing," "anti-Semitic incidents," and "ethnic intimidation" together under the umbrella term "hate crimes." Advocates, principally the ADL, who sought to gain attention for their work on the issue of criminal civil rights violations and bias crimes, found themselves within an increasingly crime-obsessed political climate where the seemingly nonequivocating language of "hate" and "crime" wielded greater persuasive power than more specific, more nuanced terms of identification.

Even for strong proponents of anti-hate-crime legislation, the term itself poses problems, particularly from a judicial standpoint. For former ADL attorney David M. Raim, who drafted the original piece of model anti-hate-crime legislation in 1981, the term "hate crimes" is a "double-edged sword [that] evokes a visceral negative reaction, something a society should do something about. But, people have a right to hate as long as they don't act on it."[14] Similarly, Frederick M. Lawrence, a prominent legal expert on hate crimes, described the term as "a distraction." In his own work, Lawrence prefers the word "bias" because, "you can hate. What is meant by hate crime is a bias motivation."[15] Both Raim's and Lawrence's reflections underscore how the word "hate," while emotionally evocative, can be misleading. Federal anti-hate-crime legislation is not intended to eradicate hatred from individual minds or from society at large. It is simply designed to increase the penalties assigned to criminal conduct that is motivated by certain prescribed biases, including bias against any religion, race, ethnicity, age group, sexual orientation, gender identity, or disability.

As its etymology suggests, the usage of the term "hate crimes" within the public sphere was premised on cultural, political, and criminological forces. All of this rhetorical maneuvering helped make hate crimes into a well-known phenomenon. But it also burdened the concept with a host of new contradictions. Advocates, academics, and victims surely participated in the process of defining hate crimes and launching the concept into broader public recognition. Unfortunately, they were ultimately unable to control the meaning of the problem or dictate the terms of news media coverage. This lack of control contributed to hate crimes' eventual sublimation to the war on crime.

HATE CRIME STATISTICS AND NEWS COVERAGE, 1986–2010

While we tend to locate the fight against hate crimes within ongoing struggles for social justice, history suggest a more immediate intimacy with the war on crime. An examination of the stark disjuncture between rates of reported hate crimes, as recorded in the Federal Bureau of Investigation's Uniform Crime Report, and rates of reporting on hate crimes in the national news media from the mid-1980s to 2010 further illustrates the historical connection between the popularity among voters and news consumers of crime fighting and broader public recognition of certain kinds of hate crimes.

The term "hate crimes" reached its peak of media prominence between 1998 and 2000. In this brief time span, the highest number of stories on the topic that included the exact phrase "hate crime(s)" were published in the *New York Times* and *Newsweek* and aired on ABC, NBC, and CBS News. In contrast, the FBI's recorded rate of hate crime victimization did not reach its to-date peak until 2001 and 2002—a full year after the news media's heaviest coverage of the issue had already waned. Significantly, as more hate crimes were being reported by the FBI after the September 11, 2001, terrorist attacks, the news media's attention drifted away from the issue and still continues to wane. Despite evidence of a national trend and a number of profoundly tragic murder cases, individual post-9/11 hate crime victims' stories were not deemed newsworthy. There has yet to be a single Arab or Muslim American hate crime victim to garner the bittersweet fame of national name recognition. For obvious political and cultural reasons, Arab and Muslim American hate crime victims did not fit into the restrictive mold of ideal-type victimhood. The process and performance of ideal hate crimes victimhood will be analyzed in greater

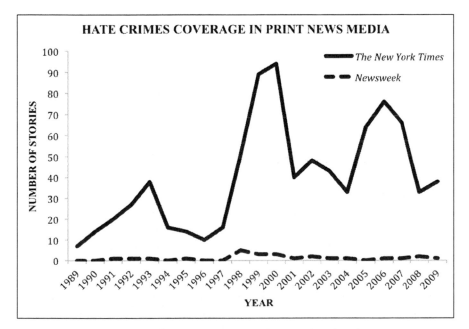

Figure 1.1 Hate crimes coverage in print news media. Based on data from LexisNexis Academic word search of "hate crimes" and/or "hate crime" both in the body of the text and as a subject term.

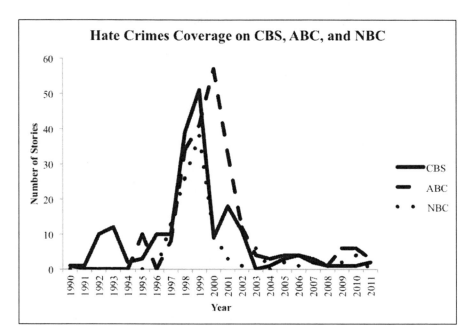

Figure 1.2 Hate crimes coverage on ABC, CBS, and NBC. Based on data from LexisNexis Academic word search of "hate crimes" and/or "hate crime" both in the body of the text and as a subject term.

depth in chapter 5. However, before delving into the specific component parts of individual hate crimes stories, it is important to note overarching national trends in reporting. Figures 1.1, 1.2, and 1.3 picture national trends in recording and reporting on hate crimes.

As both figure 1.1 and figure 1.2 illustrate, coverage of hate crimes began in earnest after the passage of the first piece of federal anti-hate-crime legislation, the Hate Crime Statistics Act (HCSA), which President George H. W. Bush signed into law on April 23, 1990. The New York Times' rate of coverage varies slightly from the overarching national pattern because the paper grants significant attention to local hate crimes. The HCSA likely inspired reporting on hate crimes for three reasons. First, by codifying the term "hate crimes" into federal law, the HCSA lent the still-questioned phrase legitimacy. Second, the law set up a national system of data collection that provided a yearly measure of the problem, which facilitated reporting on "rising rates" or "epidemics" of victimization. Finally, the law and stories that stemmed from its enforcement exuded a safe bipartisan glow. The issue applied newly popular sentencing enhancement practices, much like "three strikes you're out," and was also heralded as a symbolic victory for the anti-hate-crime movement.

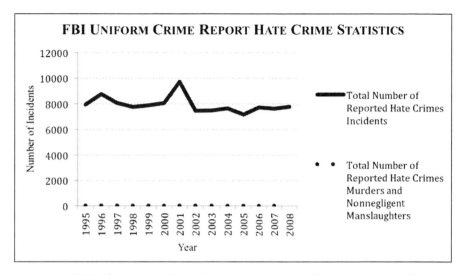

Figure 1.3 FBI Uniform Crime Report hate crime statistics. Based on data from the Federal Bureau of Investigation's Uniform Crime Report.

The charts also illustrate that while television news networks were slower to adopt the phrase "hate crimes," the number of hate crimes stories reported on in both print journalism and television news peaked at the same moment, between 1998 and 2000. Reported rates of hate crime victimization, by contrast, did not peak during the same period.

As figure 1.3 confirms, rates of reporting on hate crimes in the news media have yet to accurately mimic the reported rates of hate crimes victimization documented in the FBI's Uniform Crime Report. In 2009, the most recent year for which hate crimes statistics are available, the FBI's Uniform Crime Report counted 7,789 hate crimes offenses. In 1998, one of the peak years for hate crimes news coverage, the Uniform Crime Report counted 7,755 instances of hate crimes. Despite significantly different rates of news media coverage of hate crimes in 1998 and in 2009, the recorded rates of victimization are essentially the same. Furthermore, figure 1.3 illustrates that while hate crime murders are an annually recurring social fact in the United States (between three and twenty hate crime murders have been reported annually since 1995), they constitute but a tiny fraction of overall hate crimes victimization. In lingering over murder cases, news media coverage of hate crimes continues to ignore the majority of everyday acts of minor offending that have characterized the problem since national statistics were first compiled.

Hate crimes trends should not be analyzed in a vacuum, however. The cultural history of hate crimes, as with crime generally, is characterized by a notable divorce between the reality of recorded victimization and media attention granted to the problem. This discrepancy became particularly pronounced during the 1990s for all kinds of crime. As sociologist Barry Glassner explains in his study on the U.S. "culture of fear," "most crime rates—including those for violent crime—declined" during the 1990s. Surprisingly, as law enforcement agencies watched crime rates fall, "twenty to thirty percent of news items in city newspapers concerned crime, and close to half of the news covered on local televisions newscasts was about crime."[16] Just as Americans should have been enjoying their newly achieved victory over the worst of the crime problem, public sentiment swung with obsessive vigor in the opposite direction, thanks in part to lusty news coverage. While these incongruities may seem random, they are not. Instead, they should be understood as products of the nineties' tough-on-crime criminal justice reforms and popular culture.

While the United States has a long history of interest in crime and its control, I am using the phrase "tough on crime" to label a more discrete, contemporary set of criminal justice policies and cultural practices that began during Barry Goldwater's presidential campaign in 1964 and culminated in the sweeping reforms ushered into law during President Bill Clinton's administration, particularly the Violent Crime Control and Law Enforcement Act of 1994. Post-9/11 reforms, including the advent of the Department of Homeland Security and the Patriot Act, could well be viewed as a second tough-on-crime zenith. Pre-9/11 reforms include legislation that limits judicial discretion in criminal sentencing; the codification of and allocation of funds for victims' rights; funding for the so-called war on drugs and for policing; the privatization of the security and prison industries; and the unprecedented cultural fascination with crime, which can be seen in the popularity of television programs such as *Law & Order*, *Cops*, and *24*.[17]

The period 1998 through 2000 was not one of markedly heavy hate crime victimization. It was, however, a period during which the issues of hate crimes and anti-hate-crime legislation were both politically salient and culturally relevant. During the 1990s, the Clinton White House strongly advocated for increased federal anti-hate-crime legislation as part of an overarching expansion of the law enforcement and criminal justice industries. With the Clinton administration's attention focused on violent crime, the murders of Matthew Shepard and James Byrd Jr. and the 1999 shooting spree at a Jewish community day camp in California were very publicly prosecuted. Heavy coverage of these three incidents explains the significant peak in reporting on hate crimes that occurred between 1998 and 2000.

TOUGH-ON-CRIME TOLERANCE

As fear of crime captured the U.S. cultural imagination during the 1990s, hate crimes offered one relevant arena within which to police the boundaries of expressive bigotry. However, marking the boundaries of unacceptable expressions of bias with hyper-violent hate crimes murders does little to advance the goals of civil rights and racial justice organizations. Tracing hate crimes' etymology and its varied levels of cultural prominence binds the phenomenon to two different waves in American political culture: first, a rising fear of crime that characterized the 1990s, followed by a swelling fear of terrorism after the attacks on September 11, 2001. Between these two waves, public attention to hate crimes peaked and then receded.

The election of President Barack Obama seems to have further deflated public interest in hate crimes, or at the least introduced a new spirit of equivocation. During Obama's administration, representations of hate crimes have grown increasingly skeptical and noticeably deracialized. White-on-black murders have been supplanted by coverage of crimes committed against sexual minorities and illegal immigrants. Black hate crime victims have all but disappeared from the national stage. Instead of reporting on hate crimes, the most recent press coverage asks audiences to consider *if* the crime being reported is a hate crime in the first place. We can see evidence of this trend in coverage of the Trayvon Martin and Tyler Clementi cases where commentators were more likely to debate each crime's underlying motivation than to firmly label it a hate crime.

In their still widely cited 1998 work on the relationship between anti-hate-crime law and identity politics, sociologists James B. Jacobs and Kimberly Potter argue that understanding "why American society passed hate crime laws in the 1980s requires examining the history of the post–World War II period, especially the civil rights movement and the subsequent triumph of identity politics."[18] Jacobs and Potter are right to insist on hate crimes' historical specificity. Without the changes in American law demanded by the African American civil rights movement, anti-hate-crime legislation would have lacked legal precedent. However, Jacobs and Potter overstate the "triumph" of identity politics. During the 1990s, when hate crimes enjoyed as-yet unrepeated levels of publicity, American society perceived the problem posed by these crimes, not through the multitude of lenses proposed by identity-politics groups, but through the single, vibrant glare of crime control. When identity politics appeared within images of and narratives about hate crimes, it was often an empty, symbolic shell of prodiversity and protolerance discourse, not a proactive demand to address the grievances of specific minority constituents.

Between 1992 and 1998, Americans pointed to crime and violence as the number one problem facing the country. According to the *Sourcebook of Criminal Justice Statistics*, prior to 1992 crime had been significantly less concerning than unemployment, fear of nuclear war, the economy, and drugs.[19]

After 1992, the trend changed. Between 1993 and 2004, between 3 and 36 percent of respondents chose crime and violence as their number one most important issue for the government to address.[20] *US News & World Report* issued similar findings in their 1993 "United States News IV National Study." The study demonstrated that "seventy-three percent of respondents indicate that they believe crime is the most important or [a] very important problem facing the country."[21] Over the same time frame, when Americans were asked "What do you think are the two most important issues for the government to address?" between less than 0.5 and 2 percent of respondents chose the combined category of human, civil, and women's rights. This category never received support from more than 2 percent of respondents. It would be an almost absurd understatement to point out that fear of crime and a desire for the state to take a more active role within law enforcement and criminal justice superseded concerns about civil and minority rights during the 1990s.

The Clinton administration was well aware of the relative political capital of getting "tough on crime" when compared to issues of racial justice and civil rights. The same *US News & World Report* survey that highlighted the significance of crime to American voters also documented President Clinton's sinking job approval ratings. A memorandum sent from Ed Goeas and Dave Sackett of the Terrance Group, which conducted the survey and interpreted its findings, to *US News & World Report* explained, "President Clinton's job performance ratings continue to decline and almost half of American voters, forty-eight percent, indicate that they disapprove of the job he is doing as President."[22] Within this context, the Clinton administration tabled racial justice and focused on crime-control policies.

A memorandum sent from Senior Advisor Rahm Emanuel to White House Chief of Staff Leon Panetta on September 15, 1994, titled "Crime Planning," is illustrative. Emanuel outlined a plan that would emphasize that "crime and violence continue to have the President's complete attention."[23] The plan included recommendations that Attorney General Janet Reno make a public spectacle of the first "three-strikes" prosecution; that President Clinton visit a police station; that an announcement be made in the Rose Garden about the Top Cop program, which aimed to put 100,000 additional police officers "on the street as soon as possible"; and that the president both host a town hall meeting on *America's Most Wanted* and speak on the issue of domestic violence at a "White Church": "Sometime during the holiday season, the President should deliver a major speech focusing on community, responsibility, and family at a suburban, middle-class church."[24] On the final page of the memorandum, under the subheading "Outstanding," Emanuel included the topic "Racial Justice" and then explained, "We must determine the appropriate time to issue the President's directive to the Attorney General and the corresponding policy statement."[25] As Emanuel's memorandum makes clear, racial justice was on the president's agenda. But an "appropriate" time and specific policy had yet to be determined.

In response to the sweeping criminal justice reforms ushered in by the Clinton administration, some of which are reflected in Emanuel's memorandum quoted above, the Reverend Jesse Jackson, of the National Rainbow Coalition, wrote a personal letter to President Clinton on March 21, 1994, to "express grave concerns." "A number of current and proposed criminal laws and policies have a clear discriminatory impact on African Americans, Latinos, Native Americans, and poor people," argued Jackson. "The impact of these laws and policies is so discriminatory that crime and criminal justice have become the preeminent civil rights issue of our time."[26] As Jackson explained, not only was racial justice kept on the sidelines during the nineties' criminal justice reforms, the reforms themselves wrought fundamentally racist outcomes.

Recent works by Harvard law professor Randall Kennedy and by civil rights advocate and attorney Michelle Alexander take Jackson's argument a step further. With the rise of tough-on-crime policies and the war on drugs, Alexander argues that the criminal justice system has become the preeminent engine for the perpetuation of racial and ethnic injustice in the United States. "In the era of colorblindness," she finds, "it is no longer socially permissible to use race, explicitly, as a justification for discrimination, exclusion, and social contempt." She goes on to state forcefully that the criminal justice system, like earlier Jim Crow laws, now does the work of reinforcing and reproducing racial and ethnic inequalities: "Rather than rely on race, we use our criminal justice system to label people of color 'criminals' and then engage in all the practices we supposedly left behind."[27]

Examining the same bleak picture, Kennedy avers that "nothing more increases avoidable misery in black America than wrongheaded policies regarding the criminalization of conduct, the administration of prosecution, and the severity of punishment." Labeling mass incarceration a "disaster," Kennedy states that current criminal justice practices "starkly and disproportionately burden black communities" by limiting employment opportunities, shutting off avenues for civic engagement, and hampering family life. In sum, he asserts, "Nothing more reinforces the stigmatization of Africa Americans than their pervasive association with imprisonment and recidivism."[28] Both experts' work underscores the significant, if not insurmountable, challenge of using these same harsh criminal justice practices to alleviate safety concerns for members of historically marginalized groups, which is part of what anti-hate-crime laws seek to accomplish. Yet, even as the most recent press coverage seems to delegitimize the very concept of hate crimes, it also evidences a subtle shift away from the criminal justice excesses wrought by the war on crime, if not the excesses of the ongoing war on terror.

Discussion

The concept of hate crimes has both a material and an ideological life. While it does represent a real social problem demanding legislative remedy and law enforcement resources, it also serves, far less usefully, as a source of moral panic. Sociologist Kathleen M. Blee argues that the "extraordinary can hide the ordinary": "Spectacular hate crimes command enormous media and political attention but, in so doing, they obscure more ordinary expressions of racial violence. Racial violence comes to be understood as hate crimes, as acts of multiple shootings by avowed racists. More mundane (and perhaps more consequential) expressions of racial violence, such as institutionalized violence against racial minorities, recede into the background."[29] While scholars such as Blee have spoken out against the masking function of extreme hate crimes cases, the content of these narratives and the very real politics of their publicity have not yet been constituted as subjects in their own right. Experts have preferred to note the culture's inadequacies and then return to what Blee describes as "the background." The cultural critique has been vocalized without incorporating the work of cultural and media studies. In different terms, while a number of experts on hate crimes rail against the overexposure of certain extreme cases, the field still relies on the sensation caused by marginal white power groups to retain a sense of purpose.

In an effort to develop Blee's critique, this inquiry examines the content of the most spectacular cases and sets their production against a background of historically specific cultural work on the part of national political figures and news producers. Despite their noted powers of captivation, spectacular hate crimes serve no particular masking function in their own right. Indeed, after 2000, even the most heinous hate crime murders have garnered less and less public attention. To wit, despite a number of more contemporary and equally horrifying hate crime murders, the names Matthew Shepard and James Byrd Jr. were memorialized in the 2009 Local Law Enforcement Hate Crimes Prevention Act. Byrd and Shepard were both killed in the late 1990s. If sensationally violent hate crime murders, such as the Shepard and Byrd cases, distract from everyday acts of criminal bigotry, then that is the result of intentional human design, a historically specific phenomenon, and, arguably, an expression of insidious indifference toward members of historically marginalized groups.

Critically examining the fraught cultural politics of hate crimes reveals what Žižek describes as "a violence that sustains our very efforts to fight violence and to promote tolerance."[30] Contextualizing, historicizing, and unpacking the content of sensational hate crimes cases reveals that the moral panic surrounding them created rhetorical opportunities for national politicians and news media producers to undermine the relevance of contemporary civil rights work while capitalizing on the spectacle of violent crime. Unfortunately, the most widely distributed hate crimes stories, with their stark morality and salacious details, have potentially damning consequences for how future civil rights and racial justice endeavors will be perceived by mainstream audiences.

Ultimately, how hate crimes are perceived impacts how they are responded to. The way in which these narratives impede the likelihood of recognizing typical, everyday hate crimes suggests that a kind of symbolic violence is part of the cultural production of hate crimes in the United States. Put differently, the social harm caused by hate crimes is perpetuated by false images and faulty ideas, which will be explored in greater detail in the following chapters. Any effort to promote tolerance within a society that values post-difference ideology is itself a messy undertaking. Popular narratives about hate crimes perfectly illustrate the hidden damage of such attempts. Yet, as poet and legal scholar Kenji Yoshino claims, "Law's inability to apprehend our full human complexity means our culture must do the work."[31]

Chapter Overview

In conversation with Yoshino's argument, *Tough on Hate?* critically considers the role culture plays in the invention and elaboration of hate crimes. The book begins by explaining why and how the term "hate crimes" came to replace less sensational words that had previously been used to identify bias-motivated victimization, such as "civil rights violation," "bias-motivated crime," and "racial incident." After describing hate crimes' early social history, the book delves into the central characters and themes that originally defined the hate crimes problem for mainstream audiences of news consumers and voters. Images of the nation, perpetrators, and victims are each unpacked.

The book concludes by considering how hate crimes can be represented differently to achieve entirely different political and interpersonal objectives. Rallying inspiration from poets, performance artists, and documentary filmmakers, I end by looking carefully at examples of hate crimes stories that have been used to meaningfully raise awareness about a range of social justice issues. Despite the many pitfalls of mainstream depictions, cultural production can and should function as a useful site for challenging the hate crimes problem. When told with sociological, historical, and psychological depth, these narratives can reveal how systemic, institutional, and structural inequalities cause hate crimes. Artists and activists have successfully recuperated the "full human complexity" of telling hate crime stories that are—in their entanglement with ideas about difference, safety, marginality, and justice—necessary.

CONCLUSION

Tough on Hate? presents a case study of the cultural politics of a social problem. In representing hate crimes to mainstream audiences, news producers and legislators tap into value-laden ideas about difference, safety, belonging, and justice. These images and narratives are suggestive. They show audiences what bigotry looks like, how and when it should be punished, whom it victimizes, and how these victims' grievances should be addressed. As extreme morality tales, these representations cast the ongoing fight for social justice into a warped context where only the most violent crimes appear actionable and only victims who adhere to the gospel of post-difference ideology earn sympathy. While we tend to consider any attention paid to the issue of hate crimes a positive step toward promoting the safety of disempowered social groups, *Tough on Hate?* argues, counterintuitively, that depictions of hate crimes are often shaped by an ideological divestment from progressive definitions of social justice. These narratives hint at an emergent national disenchantment with the ideals of tolerance and diversity or, at the very least, a significant hollowing in the meaning and practice of these ideals.

The questions then become these: Can we hope to combat a problem that is hidden within its own publicity and whose very defining features are in a constant state of partisan flux? Is our collective cultural imagination capable of depicting contemporary modes of bigotry in a way that is accurate enough to allow for informed action? Even as the civil rights movement is tamed into textbooks and domesticated with grand monuments, we seem hard-pressed to simply represent, not to mention respond to, the most important and least sensational civil rights issues of our time. Institutional, systemic, and everyday acts of antiminority violence may be too subtle, too complex, too elusive, and too potentially disruptive to attract the resources required to enter into mainstream visibility. Even the limited cultural space assigned for getting "tough" on hate often carries the scent of antiminority bias, stereotype, dismissal, condescension, erasure, and invalidation.

The poet, essayist, and art critic Maggie Nelson has written, "One need not immerse oneself in horrific images or a debate about their epistemological status in order to apprehend and protest barbarities wherever they are to be found. One does, however, need to know what barbarities have taken place: there's the rub."[32] The knowing Nelson deems necessary is now of greater importance to the anti-hate-crime movement than ever. This variety of knowledge is less rooted in memorizing the gory particulars of any single hate crime (the kind of "subjective" violence Žižek pricks us to be wary of) and more about an effortful process of ethically informed witnessing, ideally a witnessing into action of the underlying "objective" violence. As the concept is increasingly dismantled, interrogated, and dismissed by critics on the right, who misrepresent how hate crime laws are actually written and enforced and who appear uninterested in learning about the experiences of disempowered social groups, those who support these laws risk allowing their efforts to slip further into demobilizing incoherency. In this context and at this moment, maintaining a public conversation about bias-motivated harm is vital. The coalitions it builds and the sane policing practices it validates remain urgently needed.

CHAPTER 2

The Invention of Hate Crimes

PERUSE ANY COLLEGE-LEVEL U.S. history textbook and you are likely to see examples of targeted violence against minority groups, including Native American removal, African slavery, and Japanese internment. In this expansive sense, hate crimes can be understood as a deeply seated, perhaps even universal, aspect of social life. Broadly, hate crimes erupt at the intersection of difference and power, which are two transhistorical, transcultural social facts.

Despite the appearance of universality, the term "hate crime" is a relatively nascent invention. Federal statues define the term "hate crime" as "a crime in which the defendant intentionally selects a victim, or in the case of a property crime, the property that is the object of the crime, because of the actual or perceived race, religion, national origin, gender, sexual orientation, gender identity, or disability of any person." This legal definition makes clear three things that are often overlooked in public discussions of hate crimes. First, hate crimes are not a separate category of criminal offense. Instead, they demarcate a particular motivation on the part of the perpetrator in his or her commission of an already criminal act. Second, the perpetrator's feelings toward and beliefs about the victim or the victim's perceived group are irrelevant. Note the absence of any mention of personal hatred. Finally, the law carefully defines a set of protected characteristics, but makes no distinction between majority and minority victims. Christians, whites, and heterosexuals are as protected under these laws as Muslims, African Americans, and homosexuals.

While it is important, as a foundation, to understand what hate crimes mean within the legislative field, it is also necessary to define hate crimes beyond law. For our current purposes, "hate crime" is defined as both a category of criminal offense and a cultural construct and legal tool used in debates over civil rights, identity politics, victims' rights, and criminal justice policy in the United States during the mid-1980s through to the present moment. Where most inquiry into the topic of hate crimes focuses on the issue's relevance to racial justice and civil rights, this chapter instead draws attention to hate crimes' connection to the 1980s and 1990s tough-on-crime zeitgeist. Rising public recognition of hate crimes during the late 1980s and 1990s coincided, not accidentally, with the overarching ascendance of both neoliberalism and crime control culture.

After first detailing early anti-hate-crime efforts at the Anti-Defamation League and the Boston Police Department, I go on to explore how hate crimes were initially defined within legislative debates and news media coverage. This move from social history into legal and cultural conversations underscores the often-overlooked cultural work national politicians and news makers put into framing hate crimes within discussions of crime and its control, opposed to more controversial debates over the continued need for justice on behalf of historically marginalized groups. Ultimately, this is a story about how early anti-hate-crime advocates' modest intentions failed to translate into mainstream definitions of the problem.

I consider the initial intentions behind anti-hate-crime law, policing, and advocacy to be brilliantly "modest" because actors in these fields sought to draw attention to the social harm caused by everyday instances of bias-motivated victimization, such as vandalism, verbal harassment, intimidation, and destruction of property. When they initiated their advocacy efforts, these actors had in mind crimes similar in severity to the act of vandalism I described in the introduction. Petty offenses of this nature generally fall below the radar of those who are not its immediate targets, who themselves bear significant psychological suffering.[1] When these kinds of crimes are publicized, the surrounding community's response is often as counterproductive, in terms of the victim's well-being and recovery, as was that of my dormitory at Smith. Inadvertently harmful denials, defensive posturing, and the desire to protect a community's reputation are hardly limited to colleges.

In its telling, this is also the story of the fraught entanglement of civil rights and crime during a period of neoliberal reforms. Narratives about hate crimes from this period proffer a useful vantage point from which to critically interrogate the marked effects of neoliberalism on ideas about crime and about difference. They also reveal the limited agency advocates exert over defining the meaning of social problems once popular culture begins to draw these problems into its skewed purview.

In the interest of challenging readers to question their current understanding of hate crimes, this chapter introduces a host of historically specific shifts in the term's meaning. The following three thematic chapters primarily address representations of hate crimes from the 1990s. The cultural history of hate crimes in the United States is largely a history of two murders from the late 1990s, the Matthew Shepard and James Byrd Jr. cases. Given the settling that has occurred within hate crimes' cultural life since the 1980s, I have organized the following chapters around an analysis of these familiar, similarly structured narratives. Before delving into an analysis of these now dominant depictions, however, it is worth taking stock of how the initial advocates within the field chose to define the problem and then situate the diminishment of these modest intentions within the rise of tough-on-crime policies and culture. Examining these early aims helps draw attention to how popular images of hate crimes have been distorted over time by national political figures and the news media in ways that limit our collective sense of culpability.

During the 1990s, mainstream audiences learned about hate crimes as a problem of stranger murder, violent street crime, and organized white supremacy, and, asymmetrically, as the final frontier in realizing our nation's color-blind destiny. Widely publicized hate crimes, the rare few that made front-page headlines and received presidential rebuke, were, until the Obama administration, consistently packaged in a tough-on-crime frame. Within this frame, hate crimes were depicted as being both more violent and less politically controversial than all empirical measures of the problem suggest. By analyzing how the problem has been defined historically outside of the mainstream's gaze, this chapter demonstrates that dominant framing practices were not inevitable. Hate crimes' tough-on-crime framing required active construction on the part of news media producers and politicians, and rhetorical compromises from the law enforcement, academic, and advocacy communities.

Until very recently, hate crimes were successfully woven into conservative law and order narratives that portray extremely deviant criminal figures and purely innocent victims and that celebrate retributive criminal justice practices, most significantly the death penalty. However, the concept of hate crimes originally grew out of a set of innovative policing practices and legal advocacy endeavors that sought to address specific patterns of low-level anti-integrationist, anti-Semitic, anti–Arab American, and, to a lesser degree, homophobic activity, both criminal and noncriminal. The lawmakers, NGOs, and law enforcement officials whose loosely organized coalition first supported anti-hate-crime legislation viewed the problem very differently than current cultural imaginings. During the 1980s, police and advocates sought to raise awareness about the harm caused by low-level bias-motivated offenses perpetrated against specific marginalized communities. Similarly, in advocating for the first federal anti-hate-crime law, the Hate Crime Statistics Act, legislators invited testimony from identity politics organizations whose representatives made distinctions between white racism and anti–white sentiment, focused on institutional racism, explained hate crimes as socially and historically rooted phenomena, and depicted these crimes' perpetrators as conformists, not as loners or extremists. Early news coverage of hate crimes also attended to misdemeanor-level violations, interethnic urban conflict, and the legislative process.

However, indications of how the issue would eventually be conflated with the different issue of murder can already be seen surfacing within legislative debates and news coverage from the early 1990s. Within these fields, hate crime murders were used to illustrate the seriousness of the problem and to lend legitimacy to legislative action and news media coverage. Even as the problem was still widely being explained in these fields in structural and historical terms, particularly violent murders and "hate groups," or white supremacist organizations, were given special, arguably detrimental, attention. Economic explanations for hate crimes were also a large part of the early debate. Where current representations depict hate crimes perpetrators as "poor white trash," career criminals, and hate group members, early economic rationales focused instead on a broader range of social concerns.

Looking back from today's political climate, I am struck by the remarkably radical progressivism that energized Reagan-era debates over hate crimes. These debates were characterized by traditional liberal imperatives, including a critique of economic inequality, attention to state histories of oppression, and the desire to fulfill the promises of the civil rights era. The distinctions and connections made within these early discussions still characterize most academic and activist work on the issue. Unfortunately, hate crimes' early social justice framing was overshadowed in the mid-1990s, at which point hate crimes became subsumed under increasingly pervasive tough-on-crime rhetoric.

The Boston Police Department's Community Disorders Unit

Policing practices in the city of Boston, specifically the work of the Community Disorders Unit (CDU), prefigured and then participated in the development of the hate crimes concept. Created in April 1978, the CDU was the first police unit in the country to take on the challenge of specializing in the investigation of bias-motivated crimes and civil rights offenses. Philadelphia, Baltimore, and New York added similar units in the early 1980s. The CDU's policies anticipated the logic of anti-hate-crime legislation and educational campaigns. As with later state and federal anti-hate-crime laws, the CDU, in partnership with the city's attorney general's office, codified legislation that enhanced penalties for low-level misdemeanors when they demonstrated a bias motivation and, in partnership with local advocacy groups, gathered and published data on these types of crimes. The CDU also produced and distributed an educational video that was shown in public school classrooms.[2]

Despite lines of symmetry between the CDU's work and later anti-hate-crime efforts, examining how the unit approached its work marks significant differences between the concept of community disorders and the concept of hate crimes. On a purely semantic level, the terms have very different connotations. Initially, the CDU used the labels "racially motivated crimes," "civil rights violations," and "community disorders incidents."[3] Unlike the term "hate crimes," the CDU's preferred lexicon included even noncriminal "incidents" and contained a sense of shared culpability. The terms listed above imply that bias-motivated incidents and crimes are an expression of underlying social tensions and shared attitudes. The community as a whole was explicitly implicated.

Rhetoric aside, the CDU was created to address a specific problem with the city's existing policing practices and widespread resistance to desegregation.[4] Before the advent of the CDU, the Boston Police Department's standard practices overlooked the patterned nature of low-level civil rights violations. Excusing crimes such as vandalism, verbal harassment, and damage to property as too small to merit investigative resources, the department had not historically recognized the role these types of offenses played in maintaining residential segregation and bolstering a negative image of the city as racially troubled. After an internal inquiry drew attention to the patterned nature of community disorders and highlighted their negative effect on the city's reputation, the CDU was formed.[5]

In yearly reports, training manuals, and internal communications with city officials, the CDU situated its discrete crime control efforts within the government's overarching interest in "racially balancing the city's housing developments," "improving outreach to the Gay and Lesbian Community," and combating interracial gang activity.[6] Within this complex picture, hate crimes were described as a "pervasive social problem" and anti-hate-crime policing and prosecution was deemed a measure of the "strength of the commonwealth's civil rights statutes" and as indicative of "the city's improved racial climate."[7] As these terms suggest, the CDU sought to improve both the city's reputation and its overarching racial climate. The unit was not conceived of as a measure of the city's toughness toward violent crime.

Accounting for low-level offenses, even noncriminal incidents, was central to the CDU's efforts and a notable rarity within urban policing. A 1987 report sent from Police Commissioner Francis Roache to Mayor Raymond L. Flynn, titled "Civil Rights Investigations Conducted by the Boston Police Department—Community Disorders Unit," is illustrative. The report explained that the unit had seen an increase in rates of victimization due in part to community support and prevention-based activities: "Public perception of the CDU as an effective and responsive arm of the police department has resulted in more citizens reporting incidents of verbal harassment or minor neighborhood problems before they escalate into seriously violent incidents."[8] In this statement, Commissioner Roache assured Mayor Flynn that the public's heightened willingness to report minor incidents was a measure of the CDU's success.

Remarking on the CDU's combined normative, symbolic, and criminal justice functions during a personal phone interview, Chuck Wexler, one of the original members of the CDU, similarly emphasized the primacy of low-level offenses. Wexler stated:

> [The CDU introduced] a role police could play and hadn't played historically. We hadn't seen these crimes for what they were. They lose significance if they are looked at as just vandalism. The goal was really to look at individual cases. The way the court system was dealing with them wasn't having a deterrent effect. You weren't going to serve real jail time. We wanted to add teeth, ninety-day sentences. This was meant to send out a message at a street level and organizationally that these crimes would be taken seriously. We wouldn't let people be threatened or pushed out— preventing integration.[9]

As Wexler emphasized, the idea of "adding teeth" is central to understanding not only the work of the CDU but early anti-hate-crime advocacy in general. The same exact phrase was echoed back to me in separate interviews with several other early advocates. As Wexler explained, the crimes themselves did not present a novel social problem. What was new was the CDU's consciousness of these crimes' negative role in preventing integration and further marginalizing minority populations. Significantly, Wexler emphasized that the CDU intended to "send out a message" that "these crimes would be taken seriously." Clearly, crimes such as murder and assault were already being taken seriously by the Boston Police Department. The added "teeth" were intended for misdemeanor-level offenses, particularly instances of vandalism.

In sum, the CDU defined hate crimes as primarily involving patterns of low-level community disorders. The formation of the CDU was, in and of itself, an act of recognition on the part of Boston's legislators and law enforcement officials. They chose to recognize that these patterns of victimization were worthy of investigative resources because they were of greater harm to victims, were reflective of overarching community values, and were enmeshed within broader shifts in the city's demography.

The Anti-Defamation League's "Model" Religious Vandalism Statute

Much like the CDU, early anti-hate-crime work at the Anti-Defamation League (ADL) sought to draw attention to low-level offenses that the organization perceived to be historically resonant and socially situated and that targeted minorities. Founded in 1913, the ADL is a legislative and educational nonprofit organization that works to combat anti-Jewish sentiment and all forms of bigotry, promote democratic ideals, and protect civil rights.[10] In 1981, the ADL became increasingly concerned with anti-Semitic vandalism and began drafting a legislative response. Working with the same balancing strategy as the organization's successful "Anti-Paramilitary Training Statute," the ADL's new statute adapted language from existing civil rights legislation and actively safeguarded First Amendment rights.[11] An internal memo sent to the regional offices in December of 1981, titled "ADL 'Model' Religious Vandalism Statute," explained, "The 'model' bill is one ADL response to the growing problem of anti-Semitic vandalism."[12] "Anti-Semitic vandalism" is a key phrase in the history of the ADL's campaign. The term "hate crimes" was not part of how the ADL defined the problem initially. The organization became increasingly concerned with the discrete issue of "anti-Semitic vandalism" after the ADL's 1979–1980 Annual Audit of Anti-Semitic Incidents reported an alarming rise in rates of victimization. In response to the audit, the ADL began drafting what would later morph into anti-hate-crime legislation. In synch with the work of the CDU, the ADL's model statute added prosecutorial teeth to sentences for low-level offenses, which traditionally would not have been properly investigated or fully punished.

Within the field of hate crimes studies, the ADL has been credited with drafting and successfully advocating for the adoption of anti-hate-crime laws. This is certainly a fair assessment of the ADL's unflagging work in this arena. However, examining the intentions behind the ADL's initial model legislation suggests that, while the ADL was successful at getting legislation codified, it was not able to control how the problem was defined in national political debates or on the nightly news thereafter. Such an investigation also reveals a deep ambivalence on the part of early advocates toward the rhetorical drama the phrase "hate crimes" exudes. The young lawyer responsible for drafting the ADL's model legislation in 1981, David M. Raim, described his work as having "modest" aspirations. Similarly, Michael Lieberman, the current director of the ADL's Civil Rights Policy Planning Center, explained during a personal interview that the initial aim of the model legislation was to underscore the seriousness of small offenses and to "teach why these crimes matter." "We count every one [in the Annual Audit of Anti-Semitic Incidents]," Lieberman explained, "because there are no insignificant hate crimes."[13] As with Wexler's description of the CDU's work, Lieberman's statement highlights the ADL's commitment to raising awareness about crimes that too often go unreported outside of the victim's psyche. The ADL's model legislation was written with the intention of raising awareness about misdemeanor-level bias crimes and incidents.

During an interview in the spring of 2008 held in his downtown Washington, D.C., office, I asked Raim to describe how the ADL defined the problem initially. Considering the contemporary conflation of hate crimes with grisly murders, I wanted to know if the ADL had these types of extreme cases in mind when they set out to define this new policy arena in the early 1980s. With an original copy of the model statute resting on a table between us, Raim explained, "That's not what the issue was. We were dealing with cemetery desecrations and swastika daubing. None of the more serious crimes were in there. The thought was those activities were punished enough by the law as is. This was trying to make low-level offenses, misdemeanors, into felonies." Further drawing attention to the ADL's lack of interest in violent crime, Raim emphasized that the model statue was "much more aimed at the less serious crimes."

As Raim pointed to the section of the statute that listed offences, I paused my note taking to study the list's details. "The only one that involves touching someone," Raim noted, "is assault."[14] Indeed, the model statute lists "criminal trespass, criminal mischief, harassment, menacing, assault and/or any other appropriate statutorily proscribed criminal conduct."[15] Murder was not included.

Raim further explained the decision to exclude murder as follows:

> The idea was not to add thirty more years to a murder conviction or send someone to the chair. It was to take crime that didn't have much effect on the perpetrator and give the prosecution some teeth. If you look at the audit, it is all about low level offenses. No legislation is going to deal with the psychopaths. These kinds of crimes, lynchings, brutal beatings, don't affect most people in everyday life. It is aimed at dealing with the kinds of situations people encounter every day, slurs written on doors or in cemeteries. Crime that otherwise wouldn't get investigated or prosecuted because they are third-degree misdemeanors.[16]

As this statement eloquently captures, the most important lesson I learned from speaking with Raim was that the ADL's model statute was intended to affect everyday interactions. The ADL was moved to action due to its leadership's deeply felt conviction that even the pettiest, most mundane, routine bias-motivated unpleasantries undermine the quality of life and impede the pursuit of happiness for members of historically marginalized groups. Sensational, media-magnet murders and psychopathic brutalities were already taken seriously enough by the criminal justice system. While undeniably awful, these kinds of spectacular killings were somewhat beside the point.

A second key lesson from the ADL's early efforts is the necessity of acknowledging the impact of the past on current social relations that produce hate crimes, what might be described as maintaining a historical and sociological consciousness. As much as it focused on mobilizing a legislative response to contemporary bias-motivated misdemeanors, the ADL also had educational aims. The ADL sought to connect the problem of hate crimes with broader historical patterns of victimization, exclusion, and persecution. An internal report written by the organization's Civil Rights Division in 1990 explained that "the ADL's decision to draft hate crime legislation stemmed from a recognition that crimes motivated by bias have a special emotional and psychological impact on the victim and the victim's community, particularly when that community has previously faced a history of persecution and discrimination."[17] According to this statement, the "special" harm caused by hate crimes is bound to historic patterns of victimization. In this framework, hate crimes are a signifying remainder; they call attention to the lingering insult of past prejudices.

Significantly, the ADL, in line with the CDU, focused its initial efforts on low-level, socially nested patterns of antiminority victimization. Both organizations were animated by a desire to draw previously overlooked incidents into the domains of both legislative accountability and public education. In this early phase, the phrase "hate crimes" had not yet gained currency, and murder was excluded from the definition of the problem.

FEDERAL LEGISLATIVE DEBATES: 1985–1988

Much like the ADL and CDU, federal legislative hearings from the 1980s defined hate crimes as a minority justice issue with deep historical and social roots. After the Hate Crime Statistics Act was first introduced in 1985, the House of Representatives held a series of hearings on different aspects of bias crime. These hearings, which were precursors to the hate crimes hearings held in 1988, included *Crimes Against Religious Practices and Property*, held on May 16 and June 19, 1985; *Anti-Gay Violence*, held on October 9, 1986; *Ethnically Motivated Violence Against Arab-Americans*, held on July 16, 1986; and *Racially Motivated Violence*, held on May 11 and July 12, 1988. Each of these hearings was held before the House of Representatives House Committee on the Judiciary, Subcommittee on Criminal Justice, which was chaired by Representative John Conyers Jr. (D, MI). On a similar theme, the House of Representatives Select Committee on Children, Youth, and Families also held hearings on *Race Relations and Adolescents: Coping with New Realities*, on March 27, 1987. On July 12, 1988, less than a month after the hearings on *Racially Motivated Violence*, the Senate Subcommittee on Criminal Justice held hearings on the Hate Crime Statistics Act. As the rosters attest, the first hearings on federal anti-hate-crime legislation brought together largely the same group of legislators, advocates, academics, and law enforcement officials that had gathered for the previous hearings. The 1988 hate crime hearings drew together a range of related, but not entirely analogous, issues that were already of interest to liberal and moderate legislators and a number of advocacy groups.

The federal hearings from the 1980s, listed above, stand out within the cultural history of hate crimes because of their progressive political content and fixed attention on bigotry's historical roots and social contexts. Overall, the hearings offered a temporary haven for pro–civil and minority rights legislators within an otherwise hostile political climate. A general tone of resigned combativeness pervaded the hearings. Legislators and the experts they invited to testify spoke nostalgically about the Kerner Commission and vociferously critiqued President Ronald Reagan's anti–civil rights policies. The discussion of violence and crime reads as an attempt to create an otherwise absent urgency around racial justice issues, which expansively included, to name but a few, reparations for slavery, improved public education, and expanded affirmative action measures. The overarching argument was that bias-motivated violence should be understood as one of many nasty side effects of the state's systematic neglect of social programs and substandard enforcement of civil rights laws.

John Weiss, of the National Institute Against Prejudice and Violence, focused his explanation on economic inequality: "Until the economic disparities in this country are rectified and until we provide for basic needs such as housing and employment, it is impossible for us to deal effectively with intergroup tensions. These factors create a barrier to educating youth, to dispelling ignorance and fear and anger, which erupt into violence. It is a problem that requires serious attention and a commitment of resources."[18] As Weiss's testimony highlights, root cause or structural arguments were the norm at these hearings. In more specific terms, participants in these hearings drew distinctions between white racism and anti-white bias; depicted hate crimes perpetrators as socially integrated; situated hate crimes within broad social, political, and cultural climates; critiqued the Reagan administration, the media, and the law enforcement industry; and articulated sweeping proposals for social change. The most salient intention motivating these hearings was to draw attention to the continued need for direct state action to remedy injustice toward historically marginalized groups.

In defining hate crimes as socially entrenched phenomena, participants in these hearings were careful to make clear distinctions between white racism and anti-white prejudice. During the hearings on *Racially Motivated Violence* in 1988, Congressman George W. Gekas (R, PA) paused the proceedings to request a general definition of racism:

MR. GEKAS: How should we begin with the definition of racism? And how do you deal with the fact that there are whites who are victims of minority racists acts, if you will?

REVEREND CHAVIS: Racism is defined as racial prejudice plus power.

MR. GEKAS: Plus what?

REVEREND CHAVIS: Plus power. Racial prejudice plus power, there has been a lot of discussion about reverse racism and all that stuff. We don't believe that a person who is powerless can commit racism.

MR. WILSON: [reads the *Random House Dictionary* definition of racism out loud to the committee] In that definition we would agree that in this society minorities cannot be racists.[19]

With no vocal dissent on the record, the participants in this hearing felt that crimes against whites that demonstrated a bias motivation should be recorded along with other hate crimes statistics. But they were unanimously in agreement that these kinds of crimes should not be labeled as racist. As with the other hearings from the 1980s, at this hearing hate crime was perceived to be a social problem that disproportionally victimized members of historically marginalized groups.

Beyond marking differences between white racism and anti-white bias, participants in these hearings began from the supposition that perpetrators were "normal." As the Reverend C. T. Vivian, of the Center for Democratic Renewal, argued, "Many of the perpetrators are well socialized within their communities and [their crimes] reflect the racial tensions that already exist in these communities."[20] "People who commit hate crimes," stated Eugene S. Mornell, executive director of the L.A. Commission on Human Rights, "are acting out the feelings of a larger group."[21] Developing a similar claim, John Weiss noted the importance of not overemphasizing the role of hate groups: "Most of the crimes in this country of this nature are committed by our neighbors and our neighbors' children. This is a pervasive problem, which is not something that we can address by just looking at hate groups. Doing so diverts us from the attention that the problem deserves."[22]

Read together, these statements form an image of hate crimes perpetrators as ordinary, if youthful and unruly, members of bigoted communities—a picture that contemporary research on the psychological profile of hate crime perpetrators has repeatedly confirmed.[23] The belief that antiminority sentiment was a pervasive, contemporary social fact led many of the participants in these hearings to define the problem in terms of political, cultural, and historical contexts. Importantly, as Weiss emphasized, the problem of hate crimes was viewed as both different from and more detrimental than organized white supremacy, or "hate groups." Within these hearings, hate crimes were primarily understood as one, albeit extreme, expression of diffuse social tensions, a hostile political and cultural climate, state histories of oppression, and as one manifestation of structural social problems.

Where contemporary hate crimes discourse tends to be either ahistorical or antihistorical, during the 1980s narratives about hate crimes instead took a notably long view: during the *Race Relations and Adolescents* hearings in 1987, James Comer traced contemporary racial violence back to slavery in colonial America;[24] during the Hate Crime Statistics Act hearings in 1988, William Yoshino, the Midwestern regional director of the Japanese American Citizens

League, detailed an extended history of violence against Asians starting in the 1850s;[25] during the *Ethnically Motivated Violence Against Arab-Americans* hearings in 1986, former senator and then director of the Arab-American Anti-Discrimination Committee James Abourezk traced the history of anti-Arab discrimination back to the Crusades;[26] and during the *Anti-Gay Violence* hearings in 1986, Diana Christensen, director of the Community United Against Violence in San Francisco, connected contemporary anti-gay violence with a history of violence against homosexuals starting in the Middle Ages.[27] As these examples show, historic patterns of oppression were deemed useful for understanding the problem of hate crimes during legislative debates in the 1980s.

Beyond using historical explanations, participants in these hearings also drew on a wide range of social, political, and cultural factors in explaining the problem posed by hate crimes. "Apart from their tragic personal significance," stated Senator George Miller (D, CA) during hearings on *Race Relations and Adolescents* in 1987, "incidents of racial antipathy are important for what they tell us about larger economic and demographic trends in our society and for what they signal about the environments in which our children are growing up to adulthood."[28] "We will have failed in our real responsibilities," implored the Reverend C. T. Vivian during hearings on *Racially Motivated Violence* in 1988, "if we attempt to address the issue of racist violence without consideration to the economic and social factors which contribute to the spontaneous continuance of racism."[29] During the same hearings, the Reverend Benjamin Hooks, the executive director of the NAACP for Maryland, situated racial violence within a political climate that had become openly hostile to minority rights. "The assault against affirmative action, the cry that enough has been done for minorities, that women's rights have been overdone," Hooks argued, "I think we have had, in the last seven and a half years, the creation of a climate that, while not designed specifically to foster racial violence, creates a tension."[30] Gregory M. Herek, of the American Psychological Association, made a similar argument with regard to homophobic violence during hearings on *Anti-Gay Violence* in 1986:

> Violence is only one manifestation of the larger problem of prejudice and hostility directed towards the estimated 20 million homosexual persons in American society. The term "homophobia" has come to be used to describe this phenomenon. The hostility, fear, and ignorance of most Americans reflect our society's institutional homophobia—anti-gay ideologies prevalent in our Government, our schools, our churches, and our mass media. These societal institutions effectively create a cultural climate in which individual expressions of homophobia, including violence, are tolerated or even encouraged.[31]

As Herek's statement makes clear, within these hearings, hate crimes were perceived to be only one expression of a normative social climate that discriminated against sexual minorities.

Matching Senator Miller, the Reverend Vivian, the Reverend Hooks, and Herek's historical and sociological depth, Congressmen John Conyers Jr. opened the hearing on *Racially Motivated Violence* in 1988 with the following remarks on the legacy of slavery:

> Now everybody knows what the problem is: How do you extirpate racial hatred from people and groups? How do you deal with a problem so deeply embedded in the law enforcement and criminal justice system itself—indeed, in the political system in America? How do we move from what might be regarded as this short, 200-year history of the Nation, to move from the status of slaves as property to the real question of full citizenship? That is really the backdrop of what it is we are examining.[32]

Congressmen Conyers's insistence that "everybody knows" that the problem of hate crimes is fundamentally bound up with problems within the law enforcement, criminal justice, and political systems in America is itself telling. Within these debates, hate crimes were, with remarkable degrees of consensus, perceived to be an aggressive reflection of vast social problems. The educational system, religion, and the media were all held accountable for what was perceived to be an escalating national hate crimes problem, which was itself only one severe reflection of widespread bias against members of historically marginalized groups.

Acknowledging that hate crimes were nested within overarching structural problems, speakers at these hearings critiqued powerful social institutions and agents, including the Reagan administration, the media, and the law enforcement and criminal justice systems. "A direct orchestrated racist attack against people of Arab descent," stated former senator James G. Abourezk, "has been joined in by politicians, by members of the media, by the film industry, and on and on, culminating in what we see today."[33] Later, Abourezk added, "Politicians and opinion leaders can leave an atmosphere of permissiveness with regard to violence against certain groups by how they react to that violence."[34] James Comer lamented, "Too many leaders have played groups against each other for political, economic, and social gain rather than address a national problem."[35] "The official response to antigay violence has been disappointing thus far," noted Kevin Berrill, of the American Psychological Association, "by permitting discrimination, the Federal Government actually facilitates violence against gay people by inhibiting them from reporting to the police and seeking legal redress."[36] Each of the speakers quoted above bound the problem of hate crimes to the actions of empowered social actors and institutions.

Focusing attention on the Reagan administration, Congressman Nick Joe Rahall (D, WV) posited that a wave of "Ramboism" was legitimizing violence against Arab Americans. "We are now confronted with a wave of anti-Arab hysteria which is fueled daily by the media in this country," stated Congressman Rahall. "[It is] fueled by the President and members of the Administration."[37] Ronald L. Kuby, of the Center for Constitutional Rights in New York, made a similar argument with regard to racially motivated police brutality. "Racist violence and other forms of racial discrimination in law enforcement are not the most prevalent type of hate crime in this country, but I do think they are the most serious," stated Kuby. "I believe, [there is] a conscious disregard on behalf of the Reagan Administration for civil rights and civil liberties generally and that certainly extends to failure to prosecute police agencies and individual policemen for excesses and attacks committed in the course of enforcement of the law."[38] As both Kuby's and Rahall's comments make clear, the Reagan administration was considered to be part of the hate crimes problem.

The structural, institutional critiques that were circulated widely within these hearings were matched with equally expansive calls for social change. The more radical Democrats and advocates who participated in these hearings focused blame directly on the nation's political leadership and cultural climate. Meanwhile, individual criminal culpability was relegated to the sidelines. Turning the spotlight of blame on the state and away from specific criminal figures can be understood as one means of legitimizing a particular corrective path, one that sought sweeping, liberal social changes, as opposed to discrete criminal justice reforms. "I think there's a lot of evidence today that we have become separate and unequal societies in a pretty profound way," observed Gary Orfield, of the National Desegregation Research Project. "We have to make a national effort to transfer resources and skills and commit to upgrading minority institutions . . . and we really have to have a serious attack on the urban color line."[39] During the same hearings, Comer called attention to the role of history and education in combating hate crimes. "It is necessary to provide all Americans with the knowledge base necessary to understand past race relations problems and current opportunities," Comer argued, "and a program is needed to compensate for the adverse conditions of the past."[40] In equally substantive terms, David Wertheimer, the executive director of the New York City Gay and Lesbian Anti-Violence Project, connected the fight against hate crimes with pending legislation extending civil rights to homosexuals: "I would encourage advocacy on behalf of the national gay and lesbian rights bill that has been before congress for a number of years. In terms of anti-gay and anti-lesbian violence, this is a very important piece of legislation. A statement from the Congress of the United States saying that people should not be discriminated against because they are gay or lesbian will enable more people to come forward when they are attacked."[41] As Wertheimer's, Orfield's, and Comer's comments underscore, in the context of these early legislative debates, hate crime was not viewed as an isolated criminal justice problem. Education, reparations, civil rights legislation, affirmative action, and residential desegregation were all considered necessary remedies.

Put simply, participants in these hearings consistently argued that addressing the hate crimes problem required both a substantial investment of state resources and sweeping social, cultural, and legislative changes. Significant state-funded, state-mandated minority justice measures were needed to combat the hate crimes problem. Early print news media accounts that used the term "hate crimes" picked up on some of these more radical ideas, but filtered them through both sensational and skeptical lenses.

EARLY PRINT NEWS MEDIA COVERAGE OF "SO-CALLED HATE CRIMES": 1960–1991

The print news media's early coverage of hate crimes—or "so-called hate crimes," as they tended to be labeled until the 1990s—offered similarly contextual, if noticeably less radical, explanations for the problem. Coverage from the 1980s tended to focus on cases that were not exclusively murders, on the legislative process itself, and considered hate crimes within a context of shifting economic realities. It is possible to identify three overlapping waves within early news coverage of hate crimes. Wave 1 focused primarily on the issue of statistics gathering legislation. This coverage reported on the debates over whether or not legally mandating the collection of statistics on rates of reported bias-motivated crimes and incidents was necessary and constitutional. Wave 2 continued the discussion of anti-hate-crime legislation and, in addition, applied the term to incidents of interethnic, working-class urban conflict. This wave was characterized by economic rationales, which situated hate crimes within the context of deindustrialization and urban intercultural tension. Wave 3 marked a significant turning point in the cultural history of hate crimes. By the end of the 1980s, as wave 3 rose, the issue of hate crimes had become synonymous with the issues of violent crime, stranger murder, and organized white supremacy.

Unlike contemporary news coverage of hate crimes, journalism from the 1980s tended to define hate crimes in terms of minor violations and noncriminal incidents. This definitional direction mirrored the dominant frame in law enforcement and advocacy at the time. For example, in a *Baltimore Sun* article, published on January 11, 1984, the hate crimes being considered for enhanced penalties did not include physical contact: "Attacks against black families that prompted the legislation included 'KKK' being painted on a front door, garbage being dumped on a front lawn, tire slashings, egg splattered on doors and windows, and racially tinged name-calling."[42] It is worth noting the inclusion of noncriminal activities on this list and the absence of violent crime altogether.

Similarly, journalist Lena Williams, writing for the *New York Times* on April 5, 1987, explained the need for anti-hate-crime legislation by drawing attention to a range of low-level bias-motivated offenses: "Race-related assaults are often recorded simply as assaults, cross burnings are variously categorized as malicious mischief, vandalism or burning without a permit. Swastika paintings are often categorized as graffiti incidents or mischief."[43] Developing a similar stance, journalist Todd S. Purdum reported for the *New York Times* in November 1987 that "New York City's Bias Incident Investigating Unit [started] in response to a wave of anti-Semitic vandalism,"[44] and that "in the first three months of 1987, 191 complaints of racial or ethnic bias, ranging from assaults and anonymous phone calls to verbal slurs, vandalism, and other acts were reported to the police."[45] As these examples highlight, coverage of the debate over anti-hate-crime legislation during the 1980s retained a sense of the significance of low-level offending to the coherency of the issue as a whole.

Within these first two waves of hate crimes news coverage, demands for structural social change and economic rationales were given voice, as were dismissive statements by the Reagan administration. Journalist Colman McCarthy, in his July 14, 1984, article on bias-crime policing in the city of Boston, quoted Mayor Raymond Flynn arguing that combating the sources of intergroup animus was a state responsibility: "[It is] a responsibility of government to bring people together [and] to work for the common good on issues like racial harmony, housing, hunger, and unemployment."[46] In contrast to this progressive pro-state stance, President Reagan was reported to have stated that if Democratic legislators wanted a record of rates of bias-motivated victimization, they should save clippings from newspapers and compile their own data. "Reagan Administration officials said that it would be difficult to include 'hate crime' . . . in the FBI's national crime statistics," detailed the National Desk at the *Los Angeles Times* on March 22, 1985: "[Reagan administration officials] suggested that Congress collect newspaper clippings to obtain such information."[47] The sharp contrast between these two statements begins to reveal the underlying debates over state power and economic policy at play within the more discrete discussion of anti-hate-crime legislation. It also illuminates the political challenges anti-hate-crime advocates confronted.

As described previously, the Reagan administration's push toward neoliberal economic policies was writ large over how hate crimes were framed in mainstream print journalism during the late 1980s. The intergroup ramifications of the 1980s economic shifts were detailed most explicitly in the *Wall Street Journal's* limited coverage of hate crimes. In a 1986 article, the *Journal* quoted a criminal lawyer who explained that "Asian bashing" was the result of "the poor scrambling over the same scarce resources."[48] In a similar article, also from 1986, the *Journal* posited several possible factors that might explain the "apparent rise in 'hate' crimes"; "one of the reasons cited by human relations experts for the worrisome trend is the depressed economy in some regions."[49] Within this framework, hate crimes perpetrators were synonymous with the poor.

As the then head of New Jersey's Bias Crime Office, Paul Goldenberg, explained, "A lack of self-esteem and identity [are to blame] for the increase in the number of juveniles involved in bias crimes. When people are out of work, they tend to vent their frustrations and anger on other groups of people, often in front of their children. The youth, in some cases, act out their parents' anger and fears by scapegoating on other people, especially minorities."[50] In this statement, Goldenberg contextualized the rising rates of hate crime in New Jersey within the parameters of white working-class resentments and the modes of juvenile delinquency that grow out of cultures of poverty. For those operating under the same suppositions about class, contagion, and criminality as Goldenberg, the issue of hate crimes was approached as both a violation of middle-class norms and an unintended consequence of shifts in the international labor market.

As the preceding examples demonstrate, neoliberal state policy and popular thought affected how hate crimes were understood. In this context, the condemnation of the individual hate crimes perpetrator took precedent over broader structural critiques. The subtleties of mutuality and the radicalism of civil rights lost ground to tough-on-crime sentiments and neoliberal policies. The killing of Michael Griffith in Howard Beach, New York, in 1986 occurred during this moment of paradigm shift.

The Howard Beach case involved a group of young white males assaulting a group of African American teenagers in a predominantly white Queens neighborhood. The assault resulted in the death of one of the African American teenagers, Michael Griffith, who in attempting to escape his attackers accidentally ran into traffic. Reporting on this one high-profile killing illustrates the way in which the issue of hate crimes was being reframed for mass audiences during the late 1980s. Low-level offenses and statistics-gathering efforts were still being discussed within coverage of the Howard Beach case. Indeed, the case drew fresh attention to these ongoing efforts. However, the killing's notable prominence participated in facilitating a shift in public thinking about the meaning of hate crimes. Coverage of the killing reflected a new conflation of hate crimes with murder.

New York City mayor Edward I. Koch described Griffith's killing as "the most horrendous incident of violence in my nine years as mayor" and as "the worst murder in the modern era of New York because of its racial overtones."[51] During the same public statement, reported on by the *New York Times* on December 23, 1986, Mayor Koch "went on to say that he hopes the city will 'rise up in wrath' at those who perpetrated the crime." In contrast to Mayor Koch's emphasis on condemning the individual perpetrators, Alberta B. Fuentes, executive director of the New York City Commission on Civil Rights, described how the commission planned to respond to the killing. "The commission will go through the community to see what gave rise to the incident," explained Fuentes. "We work with the community so they themselves resolve the problem."[52]

As these paired statements highlight, the Howard Beach case was viewed through several, incompatible lenses. Fuentes's statement shows that the community-centered frame, utilized by the CDU and ADL, still maintained currency. But a new interest in condemning individual perpetrators was also gaining legitimacy. As state interventions, outside of law enforcement, lost political capital due to the ascendance of neoliberalism, the arena of viable political action for anti-hate-crime efforts narrowed in on the individual hate crime perpetrator and his or her singular culpability. The rhetorical field within which to make meaning of hate crimes became increasingly insular. In this newly narrowed policy arena, what hate crimes meant and how they should be responded to became decidedly less focused on social change, less insistent on shared culpability, less interested in misdemeanors, and less directly engaged with minority justice. In place of civil rights, hate crime instead became an issue of violent crime and the need for its strident control.

FROM MISDEMEANOR TO MURDER: NEOLIBERALISM, MORAL PANIC, AND HATE CRIME IN THE 1990S

Up until this point, I have been developing an argument about the comparatively radical progressive political content of hate crimes policy and rhetoric from the 1980s. However, as the preceding analysis of early news coverage demonstrates, tough-on-crime refrains were already also in circulation. Where the ADL and CDU maintained a focus on misdemeanor-level crimes and bias-motivated incidents, national legislators, those invited to testify during their hearings, and the national news media dramatized the issue of hate crimes through personal narratives about the suffering of individual murder victims and the evil of individual perpetrators. As participants in these public debates demanded new history curriculums, increased affirmative action measures, reparations for slavery, community activism, and the extension of civil rights legislation to homosexuals, they used stories about murder victims to illustrate the seriousness of the hate crimes problem.

For example, during hearings on *Anti-Gay Violence* held in 1986, Kevin Berrill, director of the Violence Project at the National Gay and Lesbian Task Force, demanded that the Reagan administration attend to the civil rights of homosexuals. But he illustrated the need for said legislation by telling the stories of "Robert from New Jersey" and "Charlie Howard." Robert's "assailants beat him, extinguished cigarettes in his face, and then tied him to the back of a truck, dragging him in tow." Charlie Howard "was thrown off a bridge to his death by three teenagers" in Maine.[53] While both murders are morally repugnant hate crimes, they are spectacular, not typical, cases. During hearings on *Racially Motivated Violence* held in 1988, participants framed the issue of hate crimes within their overarching concern about the decreased participation of racial minorities in American life. But the murder of Michael Griffith in Howard Beach, New York, was the most frequently cited example of racial violence.[54] Similarly, during the hearings on *Ethnically Motivated Violence Against Arab-Americans* in 1986, the most frequently discussed crime was the bombing murder of Alex Odeh. The killings of Vincent Chin, Alex Odeh, and Michael Griffith were highlighted in early hearings and then took center stage again during the Hate Crime Statistics Act's hearings in 1988.[55]

Within the context of the rising neoliberalism of the 1980s, these gory murder cases added an otherwise absent bipartisan urgency to the issue of hate crimes. Where the CDU and ADL were working to combat a comparatively mundane social problem, legislators' and the news media's focus on murder victims instead created a moral panic that brilliantly tapped into the historical moment's unprecedented fascination with violent crime. During the late 1980s and into the 1990s, affirmative action, liberal education reforms, and homosexual civil rights were not politically popular—to say nothing of the outlandishness of reparations for slavery under the Reagan administration.[56] "Given the atmosphere of economic, political, and cultural change that characterized the 1980s, then, the options for racial policy are rather bleak," explain social theorists Michael Omi and Howard Winant in their pioneering work on racial formation in the United States. Reflecting on neoliberalism's limiting impact on state-based minority justice reforms, Omi and Winant conclude, "The climate of anti-statism severely limited the expansion of state activity to deal with impoverishment and the invidious effect of racism in housing, education, and welfare."[57] Within neoliberal thinking about state policy and racism, homophobia, and xenophobia, graphic stories about hate crimes murder victims held out a seemingly irresistible political capital because even conservative legislators could agree that they demanded action as crimes, not as reminders that bigotry was a social problem.

But the attempt to cash in on violent crime's rising political power presented a fraught compromise for those most interested in parlaying anti-hate-crime advocacy into more substantive calls for social justice. The most significant unintended consequence of this political maneuver was the conflation of hate crimes with murder that then bound the punishment of these crimes with direct support for increasingly punitive criminal justice reforms, including mandatory minimum sentencing guidelines and the death penalty.

The mass cultural production of hate crimes in the late 1990s was part of a broader history of politicizing crime in America. In more specific terms, the marked cultural and political import of hate crimes murders during the 1990s is best understood as embroiled within the overarching shift toward neoliberal governance with its attendant popularization of tough-on-crime values. As criminologist Robert Reiner explains, "Neoliberalism, the increasing penetration of free market principles and practices to all spheres of life, is the fundamental factor underlying both the threats of crime and violence, and increasingly authoritarian control tactics."[58] Adding a historical dimension, Reiner argues that "the early 1990s saw a hardening of public and political discourse about law and order and about crime control policies."[59] As the Clinton administration took office and the Violent Crime Control and Law Enforcement Act of 1994 was introduced, a new consensus on crime control that emphasized individual criminal culpability and harsh sentencing reforms had already solidified.

Representations of hate crimes since the 1980s are located within these cultural contexts and political subtexts. The overarching shift toward neoliberalism generated cultural fascination with violent crime and wrought increasingly binary divisions between victims and criminals.[60] Both of these trends factor into the content and tone of representations of hate crimes. The increased prominence of victims and the heightened vilification of perpetrators have been attributed to a wide range of structural and economic changes, which began to gain momentum in the late 1960s. These include economic deregulation, the advent and proliferation of victimization surveys, rising crime rates, the threat of terrorism, political speech that assumed stories about victims would win votes, the media's increased interest in reporting on and fictionalizing crime, new managerialism's consumerist approach to public services, feminist victimology's ability to raise awareness about previously unrecognized populations of victims, and the production of new scholarship focused on victims' issues.[61] Overall, the 1980s and 1990s witnessed tremendous change in the climate of policy making, including criminal justice policy. Combined, these new market practices and social values heightened both the actual risk of victimization and the fear of victimization, two distinct social problems.[62]

A binary cultural division between victims and criminals was originally popularized, in part, to do the work of legitimizing increasingly putative criminal justice policies and to dramatize the desirability of expanding both the law enforcement and security industries. This victim-criminal binary characterized mainstream narratives about hate crimes until very recently and will be explored in greater depth in later chapters. As criminologist Martin Innes explains, the news media operating within these political subtexts "amplified the 'demonization' of perpetrators."[63] Inversely, the figure of the crime victim grew to iconic proportions. Consider the disturbingly glamorous images of murder victim JonBenét Ramsey, the six-year-old beauty pageant contestant who was murdered in her home in Colorado in 1996, that appeared on the covers of newspapers and magazines for years after her death. The interests of the individual victim of crime had previously been subsumed under the interests of the general public. As sociologist David Garland documents, prior to the late 1960s "individual victims featured hardly at all, other than as members of the public whose complaints triggered state action. Their interests were subsumed under the general public interest, and certainly not counter-posed to the interests of the offender."[64] Previously on the sidelines of law, politics, and culture, the victim emerged during the 1980s and 1990s as a formidable figure. In the words of criminologist A. E. Bottoms, the victim became a "powerful motif."[65] The potency of the victim motif sparked popular interest in the problem of hate crimes at the exact moment when other civil rights initiatives were being challenged.

Conclusion

The emergence of hate crimes as both a social problem and a source of moral panic overlapped temporally with the mushrooming of tough-on-crime politics. Mainstream narratives about hate crimes shared a set of cultural themes, policy concerns, and emotional tones with the period's unparalleled obsession with crime. The remaining chapters take these themes, tones, and concerns as critical focal points. As the concept of hate crimes was elaborated from local policing practices and advocacy projects to national political issue and mass media spectacle, it shifted from being a way of addressing the subtle, emotional harm caused by bias-motivated misdemeanors to yet another way of creating fear of violent crime, of marginalizing identity politics, and, most significantly, of ideologically bolstering a divestment from minority justice work.

Unlike its predecessors "community disorder," "ethnic intimidation," and "civil rights violation," which all tap into histories of state discrimination and social stereotyping, the phrase "hate crimes" seamlessly cued into the popular politicization of crime control and backlash against identity politics of the 1990s. Even staunch supporters of legislating against hate crimes equivocate on the term's dramatic inclinations. For former ADL attorney David M. Raim, the term "hate crimes" is a "double-edged sword [that] evokes a visceral negative reaction, something a society should do something about. But, people have a right to hate as long as they don't act on it."[66] Similarly, Frederick M. Lawrence, a prominent legal expert on hate crimes, described the term as "a distraction." In his own work, Lawrence prefers the word "bias" because "you can hate. What is meant by hate crime is a bias motivation. It is an act of discrimination turned violent."[67]

Both the idea of distraction, or masking, and the idea of violence are essential ingredients in understanding hate crimes' many meanings. However, the certainty of what constitutes violence needs to be unmoored. As argued here, the CDU's and ADL's early attentiveness to the subtle, interpersonal violence wrought by even the most seemingly mundane hate crimes offers one sound starting point from which to more accurately comprehend the lived reality of bias-motivated crime and to envision new, more productive, responses to the problem. In emphasizing the real harm caused by even the most everyday expressions of bias against groups that have historically been marginalized, these modest practices usefully suggest alternate ways of imagining how we, personally and socially, might better counter this kind of targeted harm.

CHAPTER 3

The Nation and
Post-Difference Politics

The prevailing common sense of the post–civil rights era is
that race is the province of an unjust, irrational ascription
and prejudice, while nation is the necessary horizon of our
hopes for color-blind justice, equality, and fair play.

—Nikhil Pal Singh, *Black Is a Country*

UNLIKE OTHER VEXING SOCIAL problems, hate crimes have
been burdened with the chore of telling us who we are as Americans. "We
can embody our values by passing hate crime laws," urged Vice President Al
Gore. "[Hate crimes are] not the American way," asserted President Bill Clinton in his 2000 State of the Union Address. More recently, President Barack
Obama posited, "At root, this isn't just about our laws, this is about who we
are as people." As these statements highlight, the fight against hate crimes is
shrouded in national mythology. This elevated rhetoric about shared values
suggests that, even when these kinds of crimes happen in the United States,
they are deemed un-American.[1]

Not only are hate crimes defined as un-American, but in marking these
boundaries the nation becomes a central character within narratives about
these crimes, taking the stage alongside perpetrators and victims. The nation
enters into hate crimes stories through two primary themes: In the first theme,
the nation plays the role of external moral agent who stands in judgment of
hate crimes and signifies the illusion of ethical consensus. These narratives
participate in the production of the myth that hate crimes are un-American.
In the second theme, the nation is positioned as the real victim of hate crimes.
In these alarmist narratives, an "epidemic" of hate crimes afflicts the nation,
which implicitly casts the fight against hate crimes as a matter of national
survival. While logically incongruous—how can the nation possibly be both
removed from and victimized by hate crimes?—many narratives simultaneously utilize both themes.

Descriptions of hate crimes being un–American and of the nation itself being victimized by these crimes can be found starting from the very beginning of the problem's public life through to current debates. Even as the historical context shifted around the issue, these themes remained remarkably fixed in their reiteration; the exact same phrases, terms, and metaphors used during congressional hearings in 1988 resurfaced unaltered in news broadcasts aired in 2012. These themes and the politics they engender appear to have hegemonic tendencies, or what social theorist Pierre Bourdieu describes as a quality of "taken-for-grantedness."[2] Yet, they are not perfectly universal. Political actors and media figures tend to reproduce this rhetoric, refuse to speak on the topic of hate crimes, or, as the case of the Reverend Jeremiah Wright highlights, accept the sundry labels of extremism.

President George W. Bush is a clear outlier. As one of the rare national political figures to oppose federal anti-hate-crime legislation prior to 2008, President Bush had a limited range of rhetorical options with which to legitimately express his stance. Instead of challenging the nationalistic rhetoric used to promote federal anti-hate-crime legislation, President Bush simply did not speak on the topic unless asked directly during public debates or in the immediate aftermath of the September 11, 2001, terrorist attacks. When unable to remain silent on the topic, President Bush framed his opposition in terms of states' rights, which left the dominant frame largely unchallenged.

Significantly, these narratives reveal that as public visibility of hate crimes increased during the late 1980s and 1990s, said publicity surprisingly created opportunities for revisionist history, assertions of American exceptionalism, and celebrations of the nation's alleged accomplishment of color-blind ideals. New scholarship on the spatial dynamics of bias-motivated victimization highlights the political utility of fictitiously locating hate crimes on the "outside" of mainstream politics and everyday life. This "handy fiction," geographer Colin Flint explains, "clouds the pervasiveness of identifying 'others' and discriminating against them."[3] As Flint's choice of the verb "clouds" suggests, the nation's aggrandizement within hate crimes discourse overrides more probing interrogations of the localized grievances of specific minority communities.

In addition to being socially constructed, spaces of hate and their proverbial inverse, spaces of tolerance, have a cultural nexus. As geographer Rini Sumartojo argues, "The notion that hate crimes and the reactions they provoke are part of the production of place is another important subject for investigation . . . such crime contributes to the ongoing struggle over place meanings."[4] Within narratives about hate crimes, the perpetual "struggle over place meanings" can be seen most clearly in images of the nation.

References to the nation are saturated in the post–civil rights era's dominant racial ideologies, most notably color blindness and its many offshoots.[5] As Nikhil Pal Singh notes in the epigraph, the nation has come to figuratively embody postracial ideals. Within depictions of hate crimes, the nation not only embodies the ideal of color blindness, but also functions as a symbolic geography onto which progress beyond identity politics, or a "post-difference politics," can be mapped. The nation's role within hate crimes narratives highlights the troubled relationship between national identity and visible expressions of bigotry.

Furthermore, the tenacity of nationalistic rhetoric underscores that a range of empowered social actors within the state apparatus and the national news media approach hate crimes as opportunities to speak out against bigotry without having to acknowledge the continued need for civil rights work. In dialogue with scholarship on new racism and racial apathy, I find this cultural tendency reveals a broader challenge to popular perceptions of both identity politics and future civil rights initiatives.[6] The desire to cover up the nations' own history of what might best be labeled "state-sponsored hate crimes" appears to take precedence over accurately depicting the nature of the problem for mainstream audiences. Unfortunately, patriotism plays a powerful role in depoliticizing bias-motivated harm.

"Intolerance Is Un-American"

In depicting hate crimes as un-American, legislators, broadcasters, journalists, and even some victims' advocates have co-opted popular figures from the African American civil rights movement, boosted American exceptionalism, and bizarrely framed the problem of hate crimes within nationalistic concern for America's continued ability to compete in the global economy. In addition to these more complex approaches, news media producers and legislators have frequently chosen the simpler strategy of personification to mark space between hate crimes and the nation. Through personification, the nation is said to have responded to the occurrence of particularly horrific hate crimes within a single emotional register: shock.

After the murder of James Byrd Jr. in Jasper, Texas, in 1998, *NBC News at Sunrise*'s Jim Cummins reported, "It was an awful hate crime that shocked the nation."[7] Two separate *CBS Evening News* reports, one by Dan Rather and one by John Robert, noted that the Byrd case had "shocked the nation."[8] Rather added that the crime was also "vicious and ugly."[9] The 1998 murder of Matthew Shepard in Laramie, Wyoming, was similarly shocking for the nation. *NBC Nightly News'* Tom Brokaw observed, "It has all the marks of a hate crime, and it has shocked the nation."[10] Mika Brzenski of *CBS Morning News* explained, "The death of Matthew Shepard shocked the nation."[11] In two different reports, Rather described Shepard's murder as "a terrible hate crime that shocked the nation."[12] After the widely publicized killings of Byrd and Shepard and the slightly less-well-publicized killing of Billy Jack Gaither, *Newsweek* reporter Daniel Pedersen wrote, "Three brutal murders have shocked the nation."[13]

Vesting the nation with a particular emotional response to hate crimes works to create the perception of moral consensus. Repeatedly stating that the nation has been "shocked" by a particular hate crime implies that the nation is figuratively removed from and ethically elevated above hate crimes. Unlike a more general negative emotion, such as anger or sadness, the term "shock" defines a state of aversion and horror. What shocks us scandalizes our sensibilities and produces a vigorous sense of disapproval. In noting shock, the news media sources quoted above assume that the nation is already characterized by tolerant sensibilities and has already achieved significant progress beyond the need for identity politics. These same suppositions inform how the nation has been characterized within political discourse about hate crimes.

During hearings on anti-hate-crime legislation, politicians from both sides of the aisle and those invited to testify have used the occasion to celebrate America's history, heritage, and ideals. "Hate crimes are the most subversive form of lawlessness in a democracy," testified the Reverend Charles Bergstrom during hearings on the Hate Crimes Prevention Act of 1998. "Nothing is more abhorrent to our American heritage of tolerance and community spirit."[14] During hearings on the Jena Six case in 2007, Congressman Conyers argued that hate crimes are "a stain on our nation's history."[15] In similar terms, Senator Charles Schumer spoke out against hate crimes in 1997 by arguing that "this kind of savage, senseless assault, driven by nothing but hate, strikes at the very heart of America's ideals."[16]

The Reverend Bergstrom's reference to "American heritage," Congressman Conyers's reference to "our nation's history," and Senator Schumer's reference to "America's ideals" all distance hate crimes from the nation, an act of rhetorical dissociation Senator Schumer took even further by playing on the dichotomy between savagery and civilization. Words like "stain" further accentuate the imagined distinction between our nation's clean history and the filth of hate crimes victimization. Each of these statements hinges on an idealization of the nation's past and the nation's values. Such idealization seems particularly out of place within efforts to condemn hate crimes, especially considering the relationship between these crimes and our nation's extended, extensive history of violence against minorities. This dual process of idealization and revisionist history plays out even more concretely when contemporary debates over anti-hate-crime legislation are rhetorically written into the memory of the African American civil rights movement.

CIVIL RIGHTS MEMORY

Beyond simply asserting that hate crimes are un-American, national political figures have incorporated more complex, idealized images of the nation into debates over anti-hate-crime legislation. These comprehensive narratives co-opt popular figures from the African American civil rights movement and incorporate hate crime victims into the legacy of civil rights activism. President George H. W. Bush's speech at the signing of the Hate Crime Statistics Act of 1990, Congressman Conyers's statement made during hearings on *Hate Crimes Violence* in 1999, and President Obama's statement at the enactment of the Matthew Shepard and James Byrd Jr. Hate Crime Prevention Act of 2009 all connect anti-hate-crime legislation, civil rights memory, and national identity.

On the occasion of signing into law the first piece of federal anti-hate-crime legislation, the Hate Crime Statistics Act of 1990 (HCSA), President George H.W. Bush was reminded of a memorial to Dr. Martin Luther King, Jr.: "When I first heard that this bill had passed both Houses of Congress, I thought of a photograph in the news recently. And it's of the plaza near a Montgomery, Alabama, church where Dr. Martin Luther King, Jr., preached during the '55 bus boycott. And in that plaza stands a new civil rights memorial inscribed with the names of 40 brave Americans who died in the civil rights struggle, each one the victim of a hate crime."[17] In the introduction to this speech, quoted above, President Bush naturalized the connection between anti-hate-crime legislation and the African American civil rights movement in several ways, all while claiming the "struggle" for the nation. By explaining that the bill's passage in the house evoked the photographic image of a memorial to Dr. Martin Luther King, Jr., President Bush suggested that the very synapses of his brain inevitably bound the HCSA to Dr. King's legacy. He then rebranded victims of the struggle for civil rights as both "brave Americans" and hate crimes victims. Within this framework, contemporary victims of hate crimes are conflated with civil rights era activists, who were often subject to state-sponsored brutality. President Bush's reductive classification suggests that the suffering of hate crimes victims, whose ranks now include civil rights era casualties, should be understood as a matter of national pride. Like members of the American military, each victim's trauma is reinterpreted as a patriotic act.

During hearings on *Hate Crimes Violence* held in 1999, Congressman Conyers similarly connected national identity, cultural memory of the African American civil rights movement, and federal anti-hate-crime legislation. In advocating for contemporary anti-hate-crime legislation, Conyers likened anti-hate-crime laws to anti-lynching laws: "What we are doing here today is extending, in my view, a long tradition of the civil rights organizations, particularly the NAACP. The whole notion that hate crimes should

be federalized because they go against the national grain. . . . I remember
when Roy Wilkins, the executive director of the NAACP, used to lobby Lyndon Johnson, who was then a Congressman, about hate crimes legislation.
It was called then 'The Federal Anti-Lynch Law' and when you drag someone with a truck down a road, that is a lynching, and it takes many modern
forms."[18] The image of "someone" being dragged behind a truck refers to
the 1998 murder of James Byrd Jr. in Jasper, Texas, which is one of the most
widely publicized hate crimes in the history of hate crimes reporting. In this
statement, Conyers, like President George H. W. Bush, conflated hate crimes
with earlier forms of white-on-black violence, specifically lynching. Conyers
retroactively labeled anti-lynching laws as hate crimes legislation and then
incorporated a contemporary hate crime, the Byrd murder, into the history
of lynching, thus erasing necessary distinctions between the two types of
legislation and the two distinct groups of victims. Such a distinction is necessary, not only for factual accuracy, but also because the conflation itself does
a disservice to the memory of lynching, which is still in immediate need of
redress. As historian Sherrilyn Ifill explains in her recent work on the contemporary legacy of lynching, truth and reconciliation for institutional and
state involvement in past lynchings should be a current civil rights priority.[19]
Muddling the history of lynching with hate crimes works against the likelihood of Ifill's cogent argument gaining broader recognition because institutions and the state are already, for the most part, on the right side of the hate
crimes problem.

On the occasion of signing the most recent piece of federal anti-hate-
crime legislation, President Obama similarly evoked Dr. Martin Luther King,
Jr.'s legacy. "As a nation we've come far on the journey towards a more perfect
union," stated President Obama. "In April of 1968, just one week after the
assassination of Martin Luther King, as our nation mourned in grief and
shuddered in anger, President Lyndon Johnson signed landmark civil rights
legislation. This was the first time we enshrined into law Federal protections
against crimes motivated by religious and racial hatred, the law on which
we build today."[20] While President Obama similarly emphasized progress
and naturalized the connection between the African American civil rights
movement and anti-hate-crime legislation, overall his statement struck a
different chord than President Bush's remarks. Where President Bush applauded
America's tolerant ethos, President Obama instead argued that American
history has been characterized by the struggle to "live up to our founding
ideals." However, the reference to Dr. King's assassination similarly blurred the
real differences between civil rights activists and hate crimes victims.

President Bush, Congressman Conyers, and President Obama all situated
hate crimes within the legacy of the African American civil rights movement.

This framing grants hate crimes' contemporary political advocates a potent connection to civil rights memory. However, it also conflates members of the movement with crime victims, obscures the distinction between changes in the state's own discriminatory practices and changes in criminal law, and, perhaps most problematic, imposes a false sense of stasis on the concept of bigotry. This means that widely distributed depictions of hate crimes tend to be characterized by a failure to recognize the ongoing evolution of bigotry in American history and life, which is surely a prerequisite to informed action.

AMERICAN EXCEPTIONALISM

Beyond co-opting the cultural memory of the African American civil rights movement, legislators have incorporated the idiom of American exceptionalism into their debates over anti-hate-crime legislation to achieve markedly different effects. Conservative Senator Orin Hatch (UT, R), Representative Henry J. Hyde (IL, R), and liberal Congressman Charles Schumer (NY, D) each drew on the nation's past legacy and imagined future as a means of framing the contemporary problem of hate crimes. Many speakers, including experts, legislators, law enforcement officials, academics, and victims' advocates, have evoked national ideals during the almost two-decade-long federal debate over anti-hate-crime legislation. The following quotations are representative and warrant greater attention because they were offered as opening remarks during House and Senate hearings. From this authoritative introductory position, these statements set the tone for the hearings that followed and succinctly summarized how each legislator sought to frame the overarching issue.

During hearings before the Senate Committee on the Judiciary held in 1998 to debate the Hate Crime Prevention Act, Senator Hatch presented an image of the country that served his existing sense of racial politics. "The country we have built together is the most successful multi-ethnic, multi-racial, and multi-faith nation in the history of the world, and we have reason to be proud of it," he argued. In reference to the hearing's topic, hate crimes, Hatch conceded, "There are imperfections, of course. Some have argued that hate crime arises out of the very mainstream of our society. I personally don't believe that . . . violence based on hate is unacceptable to Americans of all races, ethnicities, and religious beliefs. Unfortunately, there are some individuals in American society still consumed by hatred. If we are to continue to be proud of this great Nation of ours, we must confront these acts of violence and we must do what needs to be done to eradicate them."[21] Senator Hatch's statement utilizes American exceptionalism to frame hate crimes as a problem of individual criminal pathology and as a means of recasting the fight against these crimes in nationalistic terms. Instead of being part of an ongoing civil rights struggle, Senator Hatch casts his support for federal anti-hate-crime legislation as a matter of sustaining national pride and combating crime.

Offering opening remarks at the House of Judiciary Committee hearing on *Hate Crimes Violence* in 1999, Representative Hyde similarly used an idealized image of the nation to frame his own decision to support federal anti-hate-crime legislation, while still underscoring his disdain for contemporary civil rights endeavors. Just as Hatch emphasized American exceptionalism, Hyde focused attention on what he viewed as America's inevitable progress toward tolerance: "Discrimination has been significantly erased from the landscape of our American society. We have made great progress in coming together for the good of ourselves, our children, and our country but we are yet far from a perfect harmonious society. We still have too many events that shock the conscience of the country."[22] In this statement, Representative Hyde emphasized his belief that bigotry was a problem almost perfectly transcended. The cartographic metaphor of erasure used here suggests that "discrimination" was wiped off the surface of the American landscape. Like chalk off a blackboard, "discrimination" was merely a lingering residue without significant, current legacies. As bigotry was not a relevant contemporary concern for Representative Hyde, hate crime was instead a nifty coinage of "sociologists and [the] mass media" that he explained as "an unfortunate and offensive byproduct of a heightened consciousness of race, religion, gender, and sexual orientation."[23] Put differently, for Hyde the very idea of hate crimes reflected an "unfortunate" overgrowth in identity politics. Hyde concluded his remarks in sweeping, near biblical terms: "Despite our universal condemnation and continual attempts to stop hate crimes in America, this unspeakable behavior continues to occur. These are senseless acts of inhumanity. Let us not look away. Let us try to determine how best to root out this evil."[24]

Both Hatch's and Hyde's opening statements contain the same booming patriotism and aloof racial politics. Each draws on national imagery to craft a distinction between support for anti-hate-crime legislation and opposition to contemporary civil rights initiatives, which hinge on a willingness to acknowledge the continued significance of racism, homophobia, and xenophobia within mainstream American politics and life. For Hyde and Hatch, the nation's unified condemnation of hate crimes underscores their own perception that bigotry is no longer a relevant political concern. For Hatch, hate crimes are an "imperfection" of the few, not an indictment of the many. For Hyde, the nation's shared condemnation of hate crimes evidences his own presupposition that tolerance has already been achieved and that continued minority rights agitation, or color-aware politics, is "unfortunate" and "offensive."

While Hyde and Hatch offered idealized images of the nation's past, both of their comments also contained a more forward-looking, international angle.

Both implied that eradicating hate crimes was a matter of sustaining national pride and a necessary arena for future national action. Similarly, in his opening statement for hearings on *Bias Crimes* held in 1992 before the Subcommittee on Crime and Criminal Justice, Congressman Charles Schumer argued that hate crimes threaten the future of American exceptionalism:

> I would say to my colleagues that if America is going to be a world leader in the twenty-first century—we want to keep America number one. Democrats, Republicans, all of us want to keep America number one. Well, if we are going to be torn apart by hatred, if we are going to spend all our time, blacks fighting with whites and whites fighting with blacks, Christians fighting with Jews and Jews fighting with Christians, every group in society fighting with someone else, there are other societies beyond our borders that are going to gain on us. And so this is not simply a message of care about one another and live and let live, the great American tradition, but a message that relates to the survival of this country as the leading country of this world. But all the energy and time we spend hating one another could be productively spent toward making the country better and helping us compete.[25]

In these remarks, Congressman Schumer, like his more conservative colleagues, subsumed the problem of hate crimes within the broader, quite different problem of America's ability to sustain its international dominance.

Later in 1999, during "Remarks on the Proposed Hate Crimes Prevention Act," President Clinton made a parallel argument. Clinton noted that "America will not be able to be a force for the good abroad unless we are good at home."[26] As Schumer argued and Clinton implied, hate crimes are not "simply" an issue of caring "about one another." Instead, hate crimes present a challenge to American exceptionalism, the real issue being "the survival of this country as the leading country of this world." Congressman Schumer's and President Clinton's approach noted the nation's past dominance, while emphasizing current vulnerabilities and future threats. The nation was exceptional, but its future remained undetermined. By lifting hate crimes out of the context of civil and minority rights and reframing the issue within the less controversial context of American's global economic future, these kinds of statements target bipartisan support in a way that limits the issue's usefulness to ongoing minority justice efforts.

"AN EPIDEMIC OF HATE CRIMES IN OUR COUNTRY"

The exceptional nation can also be the afflicted nation. Language of embattlement and threat characterizes the second main theme employed to write the nation into hate crimes discourse: contagion. When the nation enters into hate crimes discourse, it tends to be either held at a moral elevation above the issue or cast in the role of victim. In each distinct scenario, the nation plays a figurative role that resists ascriptions of blame. Using epic medical rhetoric, legislators and news media producers describe hate crimes as an "epidemic," a "sickness," a "disease," and, more specifically, a "cancer." As President Clinton succinctly stated in a 1997 radio address, "They [hate crimes] are acts of violence against America itself."[27] These metaphors of attack position hate crimes as treasonous. While the news media have occasionally interrogated the language of "epidemic" as being overly alarmist, as have academics who oppose federal anti-hate-crime legislation, these metaphors continue to saturate both political discourse and the news media.[28]

When hate crimes are described as maligning the national body, the term "epidemic" is most frequently utilized. Newscasters, legislators, law enforcement officials, advocates, and academics alike use the idea of epidemic to emphasize the scope and scale of the hate crimes problem and to relate hate crimes' negative effects to the health of the nation. "America is in the grip of an epidemic," reported Jacqueline Adams for *CBS Evening News*, "an epidemic of hate."[29] "[There is] evidence of an epidemic of hate crimes in our country,"[30] stated Congressman Schumer. On May 4, 1994, the *New York Times'* National Desk quoted David M. Smith, a spokesman for the National Gay and Lesbian Task Force, who stated that violence against homosexuals had become an "out-of-control epidemic."[31] During an interview with newscaster Connie Chung, gay rights activist David Mixner claimed, "We're about to enter, it appears, another time of great struggle. We've seen it in increased epidemic of hate crimes directed towards gays and lesbians."[32] After a series of church burnings in 1996, the *Times* reported that then assistant attorney general of the Justice Department Deval Patrick said that "the nation is facing an 'epidemic of terror.'"[33] In the months after Matthew Shepard's murder, the *Times* published an op-ed piece by fiction writer David Leavitt titled simply "The Hate Epidemic."[34] More recently, in 2009, an organization called Latino Justice stated that a series of assaults on Long Island represented "an epidemic of hate crimes against Latinos."[35]

Placing a premium on the nation's health, the terms "sickness" and "disease" are also deployed to illustrate the nature of the hate crimes problem. As an unidentified female protester explained to Richard Schlesinger of *CBS Evening News*, "[Anti-gay violence] is part of—of a sickness, you know. It's just one symptom of a sickness."[36] Similarly in opening hearings on the Hate Crime Statistics Act of 1988, Senator Paul Simon (D, IL) suggested, "Where there is sickness and poison in our society, let's find out about it."[37] In broader terms, President Clinton lamented that bias-motivated violence is "the disease that seems to afflict human hearts everywhere."[38]

Occasionally, instead of the vague terms "sickness" and "disease," speakers more pointedly describe hate crimes as a "cancer." In introducing a *Dateline* special, titled "Web of Hate: Hate Sites on the Web Affect Everyone," Tom Brokaw argued, "We cannot ignore the reality that hate crimes are a fact of life in America. Some 8,000 reported every year, and now there's a powerful new way to spread this cancer."[39] "These hate crimes become a cancer," explained Zeke Sandy, the father of a hate crime victim, to the *Times'* Michael Brick. "It's a disease."[40] In an early example of this metaphor, the National Council of Churches chose to describe hate crimes as "a cancer eating away our communities and social institutions" in a report they prepared for federal hearings on hate crimes in 1988, which was read and publically discussed by the legislators leading up to the hearings.[41] In each of these statements, the term "cancer" viscerally evokes a perception of the hate crimes problem as alarming, potentially lethal, but also undiscriminating and random.

Within discussions of how hate crimes affect the nation, the words "epidemic," "sickness," and "cancer" serve multiple, discordant functions. For democratic support of anti-hate-crime legislation, the language of epidemic heightens the issue's seriousness and elevates advocacy to the level of near heroism. With the upward march of social conservatism, Republican supporters of anti-hate-crime legislation faced increasing in-party opposition. For these legislators, metaphors of contagion aim at making the issue one of universal concern, not of support for minority justice programs or homosexual lifestyles. For the news media, metaphors of sickness assist with propelling hate crime into ever more sensationalized, lucrative terrain.

While stemming from distinct motivations, metaphors of contagion consistently imply that hate crimes are a nondiscriminating, malignant force that is worthy of news coverage and of bipartisan legislative support. As pressing public health issues, epidemics and cancers present a noncontroversial call to action. Audiences of news consumers and voters are entreated to imagine anti-hate-crime advocates as brave medical experts standing on the front lines of a disease so vast that it could destroy our very civilization. This kind of epic fantasy appears to rally greater public interest than reasoned debates over the consequences of bias-motivated vandalism and harassment. Where minority justice issues can polarize, the terms "epidemic" and "cancer" both resonate deeply with Americans from across the political spectrum. Fighting cancer and combating epidemics have become all-American battles: the National Football League honors National Breast Cancer Awareness Month, pink ribbons adorn everything from cereal boxes to iPods, and concern over H1N1 vacillated between hysterical and apocalyptic—public service announcements regarding the spread of swine flu elevated hand washing to the status of national service.

Yet, the inherent political capital of these metaphors is also their limitation. The underlying problem with these seductive medical metaphors is that they suggest that the national body suffers from hate crimes victimization, not any one particular historically marginalized community. These metaphors enable politicians, newscasters, and journalists to condemn hate crimes vocally to mainstream national audiences without having to acknowledge the histories of violence and bias manifest by these crimes and without having to take stock of the continued significance of ascriptive differences, including race, religion, and sexual orientation, within American life.

As President Clinton made clear, this erasure has explicit political objectives. In a 1999 statement, he argued that "hundreds of Americans have been injured or killed, simply because of who they are. In response to this epidemic of violence, people around the country have joined me in calling on Congress to pass this important legislation . . . the nation cannot afford to wait."[42] In this quotation, Clinton explained that hate crime victims have been intentionally selected "simply because of who they are," not as minorities, but as "Americans." As hate crimes are an "epidemic" that targets "Americans," in Clinton's framework, it is the nation, not the specific victim's community, that "cannot afford to wait" for legislative action. This rhetoric operates under savvy sensibilities. The specific plight of real victims and their communities is erased and supplanted with a national community of potential victims. Given reluctance on the part of conservatives to grant "special" protections to racial and sexual minority groups, the rhetorical tactic of replacing specific minority communities with a national pool of potential victims works toward making the issue of federally legislating against hate crimes more palatable to a broader national base. While accessing this broader appeal in the interest of anti-hate-crime advocacy has proved useful, ultimately it tends to leave the underlying issues unaddressed, with a few notable exceptions.

In general, the metaphor of epidemic renders the nation as a passive victim of hate crimes. However, advocates have successfully used the same metaphors without letting mainstream America off the hook. According to Deval Patrick and David Mixner, quoted earlier in this section, the nation's affliction is rooted within the state structure and within the same overarching social "atmosphere" as mainstream America. Mixner began by noting that levels of anti-gay hate crime had increased to the point of being an "epidemic." But he concluded his statement by implicating members of the government: "We've seen the majority leader of the United States Senate compare us [homosexuals] to kleptomaniacs and sick people."[43] Like Mixner, Patrick argued that the nation was experiencing an "epidemic of terror." But he continued by explaining that the epidemic was "precipitated in part by an extreme atmosphere of racial hostility."[44] Mixner and Patrick used familiar metaphors of contagion without granting empowered social actors in the state and media immunity from the cause of the epidemic.

While these metaphors are flexible enough to accommodate a range of political messages, they still problematically overextend the existing argument used by academics, advocates, and activists that hate crimes victimization is experienced by more than just the crime's actual victim. Anti-hate-crime advocates and much of the existing scholarship on hate crimes show that these crimes demand enhanced penalties because they are often more harmful than parallel non-bias-motivated offenses. This greater harm is experienced by both the crime's original victim and the victim's community. The American Psychological Association contends that hate crimes victimization has more serious psychological effects than does non-bias-motivated victimization.[45] Furthermore, both scholarship and advocacy projects have shown that these kinds of crimes make other members of the victim's community feel more vulnerable and anxious, thus extending the harm caused by the initial incident. In the metaphors of contagion analyzed above, yet another layer of extrapolation occurs: hate crimes are represented as not only adversely affecting entire minority communities, but harmful to the nation as a whole. Suggesting that the entire nation is victimized by hate crimes makes the issue relevant to a wider audience of news consumers and voters. But in the process, we problematically lose sight of real hate crime victims and actual minority communities.

Statements made by President Clinton and by Michael Riff, during his tenure as the associate director of the New York Regional Office of the Anti-Defamation League, illustrate this slippage. "Hate or bias crimes not only have a special emotional and psychological impact on individuals and communities," explained Riff, "but carry the potential for tearing apart the fabric of our society through escalating violence and turmoil."[46] *CBS Evening News* quoted Clinton making a similar argument while advocating for anti-hate-crime legislation again in 1999. He said, "Hate crimes victimize not only the victim, but they victimize society as a whole in a special way because they contradict the very idea of America we're trying to build."[47] In Clinton's and Riff's statements, hate crimes prey on our perception of our national identity and our national ideals. The very texture of our social fabric is at stake.

Yet, as Clinton's phrase, "trying to build," illuminates, these proclamations of harm entail a degree of aspiration. The victim in these statements is not any one particular minority community or individual, but our collective ability to *invent* the nation as a space of post-difference accomplishments. The question then becomes one of compromises and consequences, of political capital and cultural visibility: Are these rhetorical tactics necessary, in the short term, to stigmatize the most brutal expressions of modern-day bigotry? Or are they part of the subtle social harm perpetrated by the rise of post-difference ideology?

DISCUSSION

The nation is not simply a character within popular narratives about hate crimes. Instead, to borrow Singh's terminology from the epigraph, the nation functions as "the necessary horizon" upon which the binding of the post–civil rights era's dominant ideas about difference, tolerance, identity politics, and racial justice are publically staged in relation to national identity. References to the nation's elevation above or affliction by hate crimes profoundly alter the meanings ascribed to this category of criminality. Describing the nation as elevated above and victimized by hate crimes promotes a false perception of moral consensus. Both themes suggest that as a nation we stand in opposition to hate crimes, *whatever* the phrase implies.

In terms of specific cultural work, these representations conjure idealized images of the nation's pasts and the nation's values, reiterate the stale narrative of national progress toward an ever "more perfect" state of tolerance, and further hollow the cultural memory of the African American civil rights movement into a narrative of triumph through criminal victimization and state rescue. In prioritizing the image of the nation within hate crimes discourse, the social, economic, political, and cultural vulnerability of minority communities as well as the lived experiences of these crimes' actual victims tend to be overlooked. Patriotic puffery accompanied by the omission of the concerns of historically marginalized groups bolsters the false perception that even within the discrete realm of bias-motivated victimization, intergroup differences, with all of their profound structural and institutional implications, are unimportant. Put differently, the images and ideas analyzed here presuppose and further normalize post-difference ideology.

While metaphorically ambidextrous, the way in which the nation is imagined within narratives about hate crimes participates in the production of a post-difference politics. As post-difference cultural products, these representations seek to define both the nation itself and the nation's imagined community of citizens as always already tolerant, if unaware of, or perhaps blind to, ascriptive differences. These representations are a surprising site within which to observe the hybridization and rampant propagation of what sociologist Tyrone Forman defines as "color-blind racism" and "racial apathy" and what sociologist Paul Wachtel terms "[racial] indifference."[48] Forman defines racial apathy as a "lack of feeling or indifference towards societal racial and ethnic inequality and lack of engagement with race-related social issues."[49]

Within Forman's framework, racial apathy is one manifestation of the post–civil rights era's dominant racial ideology: color blindness.

Color blindness nourishes racial apathy and disarticulates calls for structural social change. As sociologist Ashley W. Doane explains, color blindness is an "organized set of claims about race [that] rests on the seemingly unassailable moral foundation of 'equality,' which is the basis for its political strength."[50] "What is overlooked—or deliberately masked," argues Doane, "is the persistence of racial stratification and the ongoing role of social institutions in reproducing social inequality."[51] As a limiting discourse, color blindness allows for the public condemnation of individual racist acts and public performances of white supremacy, without recognizing the relationship between these events and systemic inequality.

Sociologists, social geographers, economists, and cultural theorists have marked out a range of consequences for racial and ethnic minorities stemming from color blindness in education, employment, housing, cultural production, and politics, including what sociologist Lorraine Kenny terms "sanctioned ignorance." Building on Kenny's concept, Forman argues that the racially apathetic's lack of empathy functions as a "strategic evasion of responsibility." He goes on to explain that "the construct of racial apathy represents a way to capture these kinds of deliberate evasions, destructive indifferences, and powerful inactions."[52] Groundless faith in reverse racism, or discrimination against white Americans on the basis of race, is perhaps the most glaring example of the racially apathetic's sanctioned ignorance.

Several scholars, including sociologists Joachim J. Savelsberg and Ryan D. King, legal theorist and human rights expert Martha Minow, and historian Sherrilyn Ifill, have observed similarly problematic patterns within hate crimes policy and memory in the United States. In a comparative article on institutional collective memories of hate and the development of anti-hate-crime laws in Germany and the United States, Savelsberg and King explain that in the United States, "the plea for the engagement against hate remains decontextualized from American life and elevated to general principles of humanity and citizenship." Savelsberg and King's analysis of American anti-hate-crime laws points to the institutional, legal, and law enforcement consequences of excusing domestic evils:

> Civil society groups who are carriers of cultural trauma were most active in American legislative processes, and they were heard. Yet, the absence of domestic group trauma in sanctioned national collective memory, in combination with a political philosophy that stresses individual rights and formal legal procedures, did not allow for the protection of particular group rights in American law. The compromise was an enumeration of

several dimensions of social organization (e.g., gender, race, sexual orientation) that establishes the protection of individuals on both sides of the dividing lines from hate crimes (e.g., whites and blacks, gay and straight persons), while simultaneously indicating to mobilized minority groups (e.g., blacks and gays) that their memory was recognized.[53]

According to King and Savelsberg, in the United States anti-hate-crime laws indicate to the minority groups that actively worked for their passage that the state's criminal justice apparatus officially recognized their traumatic histories. However, the actual legal codification of anti-hate-crime laws makes no distinctions between minority and majority groups. These laws gesture at difference, without actually acknowledging any role these differences might still play within contemporary American life. As King and Savelsberg note, American political philosophy and legal culture partially explain why anti-hate-crime legislation nods at minority interest groups without codifying or commemorating the social vulnerabilities experienced by these groups. The pervasiveness of post-difference politics contributes to the subtext within which this kind of compromise appears acceptable.

What King and Savelsberg describe as a "compromise" might better be deemed theft or, more moderately, bait and switch. Where the nation appears idealized and victimized in hate crimes discourse, these images function as a "conceptual cloak" over the everyday lived realities of hate crimes victimization and against the social, cultural, and political subtexts of these crimes. As Sherrilyn Ifill explains, conceptual cloaks "allow institutions to justify disconnection from responsibility for systemic racial and ethnic violence."[54] Ifill finds this kind of disconnect politically problematic, but psychologically ameliorative, positing, "The project of addressing institutional complicity in racial and ethnic violence is a critically important one. It can also be overwhelming. Our willingness to see racial and ethnic violence solely in terms of individual accountability may reflect our unconscious desire to reduce the project of racial reconciliation to manageable proportions."[55]

Similarly, Martha Minow argues that "the most powerful defect in the push to regulate hate crime and hate speech, however, is how such regulation detracts from other efforts to address the sources and effects of group hatred."[56] Both Minow and Ifill argue that the fight against hate crimes makes little sense when detached from institutional, systemic, state-sponsored, and historically entrenched modes of oppression. For both scholars, the desire to police hate crimes as a separate category of criminality often misses the larger point, which is that these crimes are an expression of extended histories of often state-sponsored violence against minority groups and of broader contemporary social forces.

Deflecting attention away from institutional complicity and everyday big-otry is one of popular hate crimes stories' most troubling political pitfalls for the anti-hate-crime movement. Yet, this same masking function may offer white audiences psychological relief from potentially unpleasant feelings of guilt. Given this tension, the stakes involved in the wide distribution of these narratives have less to do with hate crimes as a policy field and legal category and more to do with the status and substance of civil rights and racial justice since the 1980s. Using hate crimes as a symbolic, normative domain outside of the courtroom has produced a range of unintended consequences. In equal measures of approval and chagrin, scholars, politicians, and advocates have noted the symbolic potential of anti-hate-crime laws. Scholars who support this legislation insist that the laws serve a necessary symbolic function. As Lawrence M. Friedman, a legal scholar and hate crimes expert, explained, anti-hate-crime laws function as an "outgrowth of our legal culture"; as such, they become valuable normative tools.[57] In recognizing hate crimes as inher-ently entrenched within extended histories of oppression, discrimination, and exclusion, these scholars argue that anti-hate-crime laws are a necessary means of acknowledging the "greater harm" wrought on members of historically marginalized groups by criminal acts of bias-motivated victimization.

The most vocal academic resistance to anti-hate-crime legislation begins from the same supposition but arrives at the opposite conclusion. These scholars accuse politicians of using anti-hate-crime laws as occasions to lavish attention on a range of different minority groups that have successfully organized themselves into resource-rich interest groups. "Hate crime policies and implementation efforts are largely attempts by politicians to satisfy organized interest in competitive political systems," states political scientist Donald P. Haider-Markel. "Minority groups may push for hate crime legislation simply as a reaction to the threat," Haider-Markel argues, "but they may also use the issue as a means to expand their political agenda."[58] Within this paradigm, anti-hate-crime laws are a reflection of the excess political capital minority groups have accrued.

Both perspectives begin from the presupposition that hate crimes and the laws designed to combat them signify a broader acknowledgment of antiminority bias. While I am firmly in agreement with the first group of scholars and advocates who support federal anti-hate-crime legislation, I also see that the rhetorical patterns discussed here, which have been used to successfully advance these laws, have limited public recognition of the relationship between combating hate crimes and more holistically addressing issues of inequality. Where Haider-Markel observes an opening for minority groups to "expand their political agenda" through anti-hate-crime advocacy, I see a host of limitations. The idea that the anti-hate-crime policy field has gone too far in seeking to appease members of historically marginalized groups is flatly inaccurate within a broader cultural context.

Even as we recognize these narratives' detrimental impact on how future civil and minority rights endeavors may be perceived and responded to, it is important to note that hate crimes and the laws designed to combat them are not merely decorative or symbolic. Regardless of rhetoric, anti-hate-crime laws are made to be used. There is a growing body of evidence that these laws, when operationalized with care and vigor, meaningfully shift policing practices. Proper enforcement of anti-hate-crime laws prompts police to take seriously low-level offenses that amount to patterns of discriminatory criminal behavior.[59]

Where news coverage and political discourse focus on shocking hate crimes murders, well-informed law enforcement officials and community members still approach hate crimes as everyday, misdemeanor-level problems, which are significantly more likely to undermine the quality of residents' lives, than to end their lives. These mundane traumas are hardly what the rhetoric of nationalism and affliction draws attention to. But they are exactly what a real commitment to combating hate crimes entails.

CONCLUSION

While perhaps comforting to some, defining hate crimes as "un-American" flies in the face of everything we know about the nature of the problem. Historians, including Douglas Blackmon, Mae Ngai, and Tim Garrison, have amply documented the role of U.S. state policy in perpetrating state-sponsored hate crimes against not only the African American community, but also Native Americans, Japanese Americans, Mexican Americans, and homosexuals. Slavery, Jim Crow, Native American removal, and Japanese American internment are but a few of the starkest examples of official state policies that selectively victimized minority groups in what was at the time understood to be the nation's best interest.[60] Scholarship on contemporary hate crimes similarly situates the problem within, not against, mainstream American culture and politics. Today, many of these crimes still express the prevalent biases, prejudices, and stereotypes that divide American life.

A great deal of energy has been exerted on the part of the news media and national politicians to symbolically cordon off hate crimes from an idealized America. Given this cultural work of separation and containment, I find that the nation serves two principle functions within narratives about hate crimes. First, these narratives render national culpability and institutional complicity illogical. Second, they work against the recognition that anti-minority sentiments and discriminatory practices, including racism, homophobia, and xenophobia, continue to be pervasive forces in all facets of American life.

Without taking these contexts and subtexts into account, the very meaning of the problem loses coherence. Within the arena of racial justice and civil rights, hate crimes' transformative political potential to raise awareness about the subtle, everyday social harms experienced by historically marginalized communities dims. In the place of accurate awareness and informed action, a double helix of recognition and denial dysfunctionally spiraling back into itself remains.

CHAPTER 4

Cultural Criminalization and the Figure of the Hater

Do you find any element of humanity in him? Do you find any explanation for what happened?

—Charles Gibson inquiring about hate crime
perpetrator John William King

IN HIS FOUNDATIONAL STUDY of deviance in Puritan New England, *Wayward Puritans*, sociologist Kai Erikson explodes the seeming divide between the figure of the conformist and the figure of the deviant. "The deviant and the conformist," states Erikson, "are creatures of the same culture, inventions of the same imagination."[1] Erikson's choice of the words "invention" and "imagination" draws our attention to the layered acts of creation that produce society's images of both criminality and obedience. But "same" is the more important word, repeated twice. Erikson's sense of sameness, of shared origin and shared terrain, is perhaps the single most essential insight into understanding the figure of the American hater. As a deviant being, the hater betrays secrets about the nature of the conformity that faces him. Yet, the work of our culture seems entirely geared toward erasing any trace of the hater's sameness. The hater is invented to be expelled, interpolated, or called into being, only to be rejected. But we must ask why. Why create to punish?

The figure of the hater, or more specifically the white hate crimes perpetrator, is a creature of the post–civil rights era's distinct criminological imagination. During the 1990s, when hate crimes were becoming both a widely recognized social problem and a source of moral panic, publicity surrounding the most sensational hate crimes and these crimes' perpetrators dramatized the issue in ways that skewed its political potential and aroused public interest. The contours of the hater's public persona, the visual impression stirred by the hater's appearance, can be located firmly within the overarching national debates that characterize the post–civil rights era. As Erikson argues, deviant figures are inherently social beings.

The hater's story is that of a "new" folk devil coming into being during the ascendance of victim's rights sympathies, the institutionalization of tough-on-crime politics, the emergence of widespread belief among whites in reverse racism, and, I would argue, a significant ideological divestment from state-sponsored racial justice initiatives. I qualify "new" here because if the figure of the hater is read as a new folk devil, then it is important to observe that he, and it is almost always a *he*, arrives wearing hand-me-down clothes. Representations of haters reincarnate depictions of lynchers from the 1930s, which described members of lynch mobs as "out-of-towners" and "white trash," and of the civil rights era's most violent white villains. As journalist H. L. Mencken wrote for the *Evening Sun* on December 17, 1931, communities where lynchings had occurred had regrettably "succumbed to poor white trash."[2] Paradigmatic modern-day haters refigured these historically entrenched images of extreme racists to suit the post–civil rights era's novel identity-based formations, ideologies, and practices. Indeed, cultural fascination with this figure peaked between the late 1990s and September 11, 2001, a period of continued backlash against civil rights era achievements and before the figure of the terrorist become the national icon of evil.

Portraits of the most notorious American haters trade in dehumanizing suppositions about the character of the bigoted individual. Prominent American haters have been described varyingly as "skinheads," "cowards and nuts," "criminal thugs," transients," "troubled high school dropouts from broken homes," "ex-cons," and "dysfunctional losers."[3] As this bleak menagerie of deficiencies underscores, the figure of the hater occupies the role of peripheral evildoer. His embodiment of modern-day bigotry is made legible through the reiteration of potent stereotypes. In representing haters, the mainstream news media and national political figures perform their own tolerance by circulating familiar stereotypes about class, mental health, masculinity, and criminality.

Beyond being a historically specific cultural construct, the figure of the hater and the degradation rituals performed upon him also play an essential role in framing the problem of hate crimes within a "post-difference" worldview. The figure of the hater's very familiarity, the tropes that have come to define his strong cultural presence, convey to mainstream audiences that bigotry is an individual criminal or mental health problem that is best handled by law enforcement authorities. In conversation with new scholarship from cultural criminology and whiteness studies, this chapter argues that the figure of the hater functions as a convenient receptacle for the disposal of white guilt and as yet another folk devil caricature within the Barnumesque spectacle of American crime.

More importantly, narratives about his harsh punishment permit discussions about much thornier social issues partially to enter into the mainstream's purview. In covering the punishment of haters, the mainstream news media and politicians not only symbolically take a stand against bigotry, they also eke out enough elbow room to gesture evocatively at important social issues, like racism and homophobia, that are somewhat too challenging, too complex for sound bites, headlines, and campaign ads. All this flashy maneuvering is accomplished without the risk of actually having to detail the real issues concerning the status and treatment of historically marginalized groups, such as the ever-rising gap in wealth between white and nonwhite households or the unprecedented levels of harassment gay and lesbian teenagers are subject to while attending high school.

Most startlingly, these narratives also tend to proffer robust support for capital punishment. The most widely covered hate crimes trials from the 1990s ultimately resulted in either the application of the death penalty or its marginally being spared after victims requested a modicum of lenience. The general sentiment was that these kinds of crimes and these kinds of criminals were the reason we needed ready access to electric chairs and lethal injections. Finding support for the death penalty within stories about white-on-minority hate crimes presents a swarm of ethical and historical conundrums: On the one hand, there is a mass of evidence documenting that the death penalty itself is meted out in ways that are biased against racial and ethnic minorities. On the other hand, there is an equally substantial body of evidence documenting the failure of the criminal justice system to severely punish white offenders who perpetrate violent crimes against minorities. Public support for the death penalty in hate crimes cases both lends legitimacy to a clearly biased practice while also seeming to attempt to remedy a long history of unequal justice. As with so much of hate crimes discourse, the underlying moral principles are impossibly fraught with ambiguity and contradiction. In this muddy contest between civil rights and tough-on-crime sentiments, the hater's public punishment appears to be more a performance of post-tolerance politics than a genuine act of justice for historically marginalized groups.

THEMES AND FIGURES

This chapter moves between themes and case studies. Themes are introduced and then both illustrated and complicated by more detailed discussions of prominent American haters. The perpetrators selected for these brief case studies were the focal point of sustained news media coverage and were subject to outspoken public condemnation. These figures—namely Aaron J. McKinney, Russell A. Henderson, James Burmeister, and John William King—achieved paradigmatic status within the cultural history of hate crimes. The crimes these men committed were the most intensely covered hate crimes in the history of reporting on hate crimes. Reporting on King, McKinney, and

Henderson's crimes alone sent aggregate coverage of hate crimes to an all-time high in 1998. The mediated personas of these men draw on and reproduce the central themes, tropes, and "truisms" that have come to define the figure of the hater. Within the public sphere, these men's tattoos, trailers, and menacing courtroom presences superficially stand in for deeper understandings of the hate crimes problem.

Readers will notice that perpetrators of homophobic and racist hate crimes are the focus of this chapter, that they are not meaningfully differentiated, and that perpetrators of anti-Arab and anti-Muslim hate crimes are largely missing. This limited focus and lack of differentiation is a direct reflection of the news media's own skewed recognition of the problem.

IMAGES OF THE "WHITE TRASH" HATER

Representations of prominent haters suggest that bigotry and impoverishment are codependent. In many ways, the figure of the hater can be read as a subspecies of "poor white trash," which is a loaded term that will be explored in greater depth later in the chapter. Descriptions of haters' residences in "the poor part of town," their educational nonattainment, and their unemployment history all function as coded class markers that symbolically situate the hater within the lowest possible economic class.

Within mainstream representations, hate crimes perpetrators' living situations tend to be considered notable, particularly when these residencies reflect social isolation, spatial marginality, and poverty. For example, CBS Morning News explained that Charles Rourk and Mark Kohut, suspects in a 1993 Florida hate crime, were not "true locals, but rather displaced and disaffected."[4] In similar terms, the Wall Street Journal noted that Rourk and Kohut were "shiftless troublemakers."[5] In reference to Ronald Gay, the perpetrator of a hate crime shooting spree in Roanoke, Virginia, in 2002, which resulted in the death of one person and serious injuries to six others, Ted Koppel stated that Gay was "a drifter from out of town."[6] The words "displaced," "shiftless," and "drifter" work to create the perception of involuntary social isolation. These perpetrators are not seen as simply relocating away from their hometowns. Instead, they are described as misfits and exiles, whose fundamental rootlessness predated, and perhaps predetermined, their bigoted criminality. As these examples begin to illustrate, when the perpetrator of a well-publicized hate crime is a "drifter," a "loner," or a "hillbilly hick," these become loaded, class-coded details within the crime's narrative.[7]

Descriptions of haters' trailers similarly underscore their lower-class status. Hate crime perpetrators are often understood vis-à-vis the landscape of trailer parks. In the wake of the widely publicized 1998 killing of Matthew Shepard in Laramie, Wyoming, reporters were quick to observe that the crime's perpetrators, Aaron McKinney and Russell Henderson, lived in a trailer park in the "poor part of town." *NBC Nightly News* reported that McKinney and Henderson "lived in this mobile home on the outskirts of Laramie."[8] During a February 5, 1999, revisiting of the crime, NBC's *Dateline* elaborated, "Neither [McKinney or Henderson] was from the university; both were high school dropouts from a poor part of town."[9] Within both *NBC News* stories, McKinney and Henderson's marginal class status was situated in direct contrast to the university town's more prosperous community. Tellingly, their trailer was "on the outskirts."

Descriptions of hate crime perpetrator Mark Kohut's life in a Florida trailer park contain an even more pointed emphasis on criminal marginality. "Neighbors described him [Kohut] in interviews with sheriff's investigators as the 'mean one,'" reported Milo Geyelin for the *Wall Street Journal* on August 24, 1993. Kohut was said to have "wandered about the trailer park with a semiautomatic handgun strapped in a shoulder holster or shot at stray chickens with a crossbow. When sheriff's deputies led him away in handcuffs . . . neighbors burst into cheers."[10]

As this vignette illustrates, Kohut expressed his monstrosity within the setting of a trailer park, where his bizarrely antisocial behavior was apparently witnessed with disdain. The word "wandered" underscores Kohut's aimlessness, while the scene of his neighbors cheering his arrest further highlights his lack of social integration. Within this narrative, the space of the trailer park opens up possibilities for random unattended poultry, antiquated weaponry, and an unbridled hater. Just as the chickens and the arsenal seem at odds with popular images of suburbia, so too does the constructed image of the extreme racist mismatch cultural images of middle-class American life.

These images of externality, animated through references to trailer parks, enter onto the field of play even when hate crimes perpetrators do not themselves reside in trailers. When soldiers in North Carolina shot down an African American couple in 1995, Forrest Sawyer reported for *ABC World News* that the perpetrators "rented a room in this mobile home" to store their Nazi paraphernalia.[11] Similarly, reporting on an abduction-related hate crime in West Virginia in 2007, the *New York Times* emphasized that, while the crime's perpetrators lived in a house, the crime was committed next door in a "backwoods" and "ramshackle trailer."[12] As these examples illustrate, mobile homes, or "trailers," are used as character-building details within public understandings of who commits hate crimes. When hate crimes perpetrators do not live in, or rent, trailers, their housing situation is not deemed newsworthy.

Descriptions of hate crimes perpetrators' employment and educational attainment similarly entangle ideas about class with explications for hate crimes. "Dropout" and "unemployed" are the two most frequently used terms to describe haters' education and employment. Aaron McKinney and Russell Henderson were described as "high school dropouts."[13] Charles Rourk was said to be "a former paper-mill worker"; meanwhile the career path of his accomplice, Mark Kohut, was outside of the legal economy. "Mr. Kohut has a criminal record for selling cocaine in Illinois and for prostituting his teenage wife in Pennsylvania."[14] John William King, another prominent hate crime perpetrator, was described as having "dropped out of high school in ninth grade" to do "manual labor" before being incarcerated.[15] As these examples highlight, hate crimes perpetrators' occupations become newsworthy when they reflect underlying stereotypes about the nature of recidivism, deviance, educational nonattainment, and marginalized kinds of manual labor.

The conflation of bigoted criminality and unemployment has even overshadowed the facts of actual cases. After the killing of Vincent Chin in Detroit in 1982, newscasters and journalists described Chin's killers, Ronald Ebens and Ted Nitz, as "unemployed Detroit auto workers." During a 2000 commemoration, CNN explained that "Vincent Chin, a Chinese-American, was beaten to death by unemployed Detroit auto workers angered over Japanese car imports."[16] This same narrative appeared everywhere from congressional hearings on anti-Asian violence to speeches made by President Ronald Reagan and Jesse Jackson and again during Chin's grieving mother's appearance on *The Phil Donahue Show*. Even National Public Radio's *Morning Edition* host Alex Chadwick reported in 1992 that "ten years ago in Detroit Vincent Chin, an Asian-American, was killed by two unemployed autoworkers who apparently blamed Chin for their economic plight."[17] At the time of the attack, however, Ebens worked as a foreman for Chrysler and Nitz was a part-time student.[18]

Up until now, we have been examining how stereotypes about class participate in determining what kind of information is included within the public profile of prominent hate crimes perpetrators. Ideas about class are central to understanding why McKinney's and Kohut's trailers matter. Heavily inflected by presuppositions about class, the terms "drifter," "high school dropout," and "trailer" all perform the significant cultural work of forming an othered identity for haters. These themes combined demonstrate that the figure of the hater's symbolic estrangement from the mainstream primarily rests on the media's ability to portray him as a member of the lowest-of-the-low economic class, to ensnare him within stereotypes about "poor white trash." The figure of the hater might best be labeled, for descriptive purposes, the "white-trash hater."

Two key points can be underscored: First, these narratives highlight the symbolic intensity of classism within mainstream American culture, which has profoundly influenced images of all kinds of criminality, not just hate crimes.

Second, they also reveal how classism has been used to symbolically remove bigotry from images of mainstream America. Taking a closer look at McKinney and Henderson offers a more nuanced picture of how class operates within popular understandings of what, or who, bigotry has come to look like.

Aaron McKinney and Russell Henderson

As perpetrators of the single most widely covered hate crime in the history of hate crimes reporting, McKinney and Henderson have come to represent the figure of the hater for a wide range of different audiences. In 1999, McKinney and Henderson were convicted in the beating death of Matthew Shepard in Laramie, Wyoming. On the night of the attack, they offered to give Shepard a ride home from a local bar, the Fireside Lounge. Once Shepard was in their truck, McKinney and Henderson beat him with the butt of their gun repeatedly in the head, neck, hands, and genitals and stole his wallet and shoes. They then left him outdoors in numbing winter temperatures. Shepard, discovered the next morning by a mountain biker, was hospitalized for four days before passing. The case became a rallying call for anti-hate-crime laws, and Shepard is still widely viewed as a gay rights martyr. The perpetrators' consecutive life sentences were described as "stiff and proper."[19] McKinney and Henderson were not officially charged with committing a hate crime. Wyoming never passed state-level anti-hate-crime legislation. Despite this lack of legal legitimization, the news media, political figures, the victim's family, and advocacy groups all labeled Shepard's killing a hate crime.

Commenting on the crime in 1999, President Clinton argued, "We cannot surrender to those on the fringe of our society who lash out at those who are different."[20] The idea that Henderson and McKinney existed on the outside, or "fringe," of society spatially, economically, and ideologically was repeated throughout the news media's attempt to explain these men and the crime they committed. A *New York Times* article on the killers titled "Men Held in Beating Lived on the Fringes" sums up the public consensus that McKinney and Henderson were peripheral evils.

As described previously, McKinney's and Henderson's lack of stable employment, lack of educational attainment, and mobile home were used to mark them as despised members of the white underclass. In fuller biographies, these class-coded details were woven into story lines about the men's upbringings, personalities, and life choices. Despite the intense publicity afforded to their crime, McKinney and Henderson remain surprisingly elusive public figures. More so than for any of the other paradigmatic white hate crimes perpetrators, the news media have yet to settle on a single interpretation of McKinney's and Henderson's identities. The breadth of inconsistency is itself telling. McKinney and Henderson have been described as average hometown boys, as severe drug addicts, as volatile, as dumb, as new parents, as victims of physical and sexual abuse, as employed, and as unemployed. Yet, very few stories actually bothered to include any substantive background information on either convict. The only consistently included information concerned the men's age; they were described as "young." The next most frequently cited fact regarded their educational attainment; they were "high-school dropouts."[21] In distinguishing between the two convicts, McKinney tended to be depicted as the "ringleader" and Henderson as the "quiet follower."[22]

In the mid-October limbo between when McKinney and Henderson beat Shepard, on the night of the 6th, and when Shepard died on the 12th, the men's public image was only mildly negative. With a notable lack of apocalyptic hand wringing, *NBC News'* Soledad O'Brien reported from Laramie on October 10, 1998: "People who know them paint a picture of Henderson and McKinney that seems, if anything, small-town ordinary. Co-workers at a local fast-food restaurant describe Henderson as a good employee. He lived in a house trailer on the edge of town. There are bags of empty beer cans against the fence there. Neighbor Ward McClelland says he complained to the police at least three times of Henderson shooting fireworks and throwing bottles."[23] In this liminal moment, the noisy mess around Henderson's trailer was deemed newsworthy. But, the men were still seen as "ordinary." Henderson was even praised as a being a "good employee."

After Shepard's death, representations of the men's characters hardened into more damning forms. This shift underscores the media process of amplifying the demonization of crime perpetrators: The nature of McKinney's and Henderson's public personas had less to do with the facts of their lives before the crime than with public perception of the crime itself.[24] As the crime changed status from assault to murder, they were reborn as monstrous career criminals. Within four days of Shepard's death, *New York Times* journalist James Brooke focused his description on the men's criminal histories:

> Mr. McKinney, known around Laramie for his short temper and willingness to brawl, was awaiting sentencing for burglarizing $2,500 from a Kentucky Fried Chicken restaurant. . . . A 22 year old roofer who dropped out of high school . . . Mr. McKinney, the father of a new baby. . . . Mr. Henderson dropped out of Laramie High School, taking jobs, and most recently, repairing roofs. By the time of his arrest last week, he had committed several driving offenses and had two convictions for drunken driving.[25]

Newsweek's Joshua Hammer similarly highlighted McKinney's and Henderson's criminality. In his November 8, 1999, report on Henderson's trial,

Hammer described both men as "high-school dropouts and methamphet-amine users who worked as sometime roofers." "[They lived an] aimless exis-tence," elaborated Hammer. He concluded, "It was a life of drifting through bars and convenience stores, struggling to support their infant son in a hole-in-the-wall apartment, and snorting and smoking eight balls of crystal methamphetamine."[26]

A widely repeated description of McKinney's and Henderson's behavior at the bar where they met Shepard similarly situates their bigoted criminality within a performance of impoverishment. In an interview with *NBC Nightly News*, Fireside bartender Matt Galloway explained that after ordering a pitcher of beer, "[McKinney and Henderson] paid for it with nickels and dimes. They dug through their pockets and, you know, put the change out on the bar."[27] Galloway's description of Henderson and McKinney walking up to the bar and having to root around in their pockets for change was repeated in numer-ous news broadcasts and articles at the time, and again later in news specials and made-for-TV movies.[28] This simple, semiprivate moment was used to demonstrate McKinney's and Henderson's lack of finances, poor decision-making abilities, and faulty priorities. These character judgments were then situated within extended narratives about their "troubled" childhoods.

As *ABC News* reported in 2004, McKinney and Henderson came from "classically troubled backgrounds": "Russell Henderson was born to a teenage alcoholic and raised without a father. He saw his mother being beaten by a series of boyfriends, some of whom also assaulted Russell. Aaron McKinney's childhood, too, was less than picture-perfect. His father, a long-haul trucker, was rarely around. He eventually divorced Aaron's mother, a nurse who died when Aaron was 16, as a result of a botched surgery."[29] This discussion of Henderson's and McKinney's childhoods implies a correlation among economic deprivation, abusive parenting, and the eventuality of criminal bigotry. Even though the men openly confessed to the killing, the news media further solidified their guilt by highlighting their and their parents' failures to live up to middle-class norms of family life. In drawing attention to the absence of father figures from McKinney's and Henderson's childhoods, these widely distributed biographies suggest that the breakdown of the traditional family, with all of its veiled economic and moral implications, was perceived as a pertinent detail in forming an understanding of the crime's brutality. Class here becomes less about actual economics and more about the reproduction of stereotypes.

In the background of this grand symbolic narrative, the perpetrators' alleged homophobia withers away, simmered down to an easily dismissible, if vile, expression of only the most deprived individual criminal's mind. Active debates over the status of sexual minorities' yet-to-be-achieved full civil rights in marriage, employment, housing, and military service remain highly contentious, profoundly relevant contemporary social issues. Yet, this kind of hate crime story falsely implies, largely through classist invective, that mainstream America is not shaped by homophobia and heteronormativity.

FAILED PERFORMANCES OF MASCULINITY

As the preceding references to Mark Kohut's prostituting his "teenage wife" and Aaron McKinney's and Russell Henderson's broken homes, deadbeat dads, and illegitimate children suggest, profiles of prominent hate crimes perpetrators belabor these criminals' inadequate performances of masculinity. Haters that garner news media attention are not only killers, they are also abusive husbands, poor providers, and weaklings. The peak expression of romantic love for the most prominent hate crime perpetrators are filtered through the criminal justice system: John William King's multiple girlfriends dated him through prison letters, and Aaron McKinney's and Russell Henderson's girlfriends at the time of Shepard's murder showed their loyalty by lying to the news media and to local law enforcement officials on behalf of their boyfriends. In all three cases, the women's contributions were damning. Descriptions of hate crime murderer James Burmeister as a "weakling" reveal how the nonaccomplishment of masculinity has been woven into popular mythology about the figure of the hater.

James Burmeister

In the company of two friends, James Burmeister gunned down an African American couple out enjoying an evening walk in 1995. The killing was described as "execution style" because it seems to have been planned in advance and was committed with a degree of precision. The prosecution rallied testimony that Burmeister committed the double murder in the interest of proving himself to other racist skinheads and to earn the right to wear a spider web tattoo, which in some circles symbolizes the taking of a life. The defense argued that Burmeister's brain had been "soaking in alcohol for twelve or thirteen hours" before the attack and that, with two gallons of beer in his system, Burmeister was in a blackout state during the shootings. Burmeister was convicted of the killings and assigned a life sentence. He served the first eight years of his sentence in the state prison system. After being repeatedly attacked, he was moved into protected custody in a federal prison, were he died at the age of thirty one. An autopsy was performed, but its findings were not reported publicly.

At the time the murders were committed, Burmeister and his coconspirators were serving in the 82nd Airborne Division at Fort Bragg in Fayetteville, North Carolina. The perpetrators' military status forced the army to "look at extremism" within its ranks. The ensuing internal investigation concluded that the slaying was a "random case of racism" committed by "a tiny fringe element."[30] Published descriptions of Burmeister worked to further distance the crime's underlying values from the military's, and in turn the nation's, conscience. Reports of Burmeister's lack of masculine attributes played a central role within the strategies of rhetorical dissociation deployed by military officials and reiterated by the national news media.

In covering the case, journalists and newscasters depicted Burmeister as infatuated with white supremacist subculture, as comfortable in spaces of white poverty, and as a weakling in the military's ranks. Burmeister was "arrested in a trailer where the police found a Nazi flag, literature praising Adolf Hitler, and what police officers described as pamphlets from ultra-right-wing groups."[31] This statement emphasizes that Burmeister's racism was a part of his identity and that the physical evidence of that deviant belonging had to be materially kept apart from his military life in a trailer, instead of in the barracks. A wide range of news sources reported on the fact that Burmeister housed his racist literature and white power music in a trailer. The intense attention paid to this arguably irrelevant detail further underscores the perceived intersectionality of spaces of white poverty and white supremacy, elaborated upon in the previous section.

Beyond this merged ideological and spatial slumming, Burmeister's superiors described him to the media as a biologically predetermined loser. As CBS News' *48 Hours* reported, Burmeister was considered to be weak:

CAPT. BARKER [Burmeister's commanding officer]: The unit I was in at that time was a good, solid, tight unit.

SPENCER: But Burmeister wasn't part of it. Physically he couldn't cut it.

SPECIALIST SAVOY WILSON: He couldn't even run half a mile. Burmeister was just the—the weakest person in the unit. So we kind of pushed him away and like I said, idle hands are the devil's workshop.

SPENCER: So Burmeister found acceptance in a different quarter.

SPC. WILSON: All the weakest people in the whole unit hung out together and they all called themselves racist Nazi skinheads.[32]

In this interview, Burmeister's superiors cast him as weak, unfit, and rejected. Furthermore, they explained that Burmeister was an outcast due to his own personal failings, which in turn led to a deviant quest for acceptance within a circle of similarly inferior individuals. Within this framework, Burmeister's own character flaws both justified his social isolation on the base and explained his criminal, bigoted actions.

As one example of a paradigmatic hater, Burmeister was depicted as being genetically inferior and bound up with the trappings of white power and white trash. This report's emphasis on Burmeister's physical weakness and his rejection by fitter military males rests upon suppositions about masculinity. While all of the most prominent hate crimes perpetrators are males, they are depicted as failing to properly perform masculinity: they are not good providers, nor good fathers, nor strong, nor stoic, nor athletic. This failure, along with other inadequacies, is then written into explications of the perpetrator's motivation for committing these otherwise "unthinkable" crimes. Beyond simply noting Burmeister's physical weakness, or inept manhood, the above description connects his being a loser and a loner with his choice to join a hate group.

HATE GROUP MEMBERSHIP

Hate group membership is another pervasive theme within representations of hate crimes perpetrators. Prominent perpetrators are frequently described as "hard-core haters." Indeed, the hate crimes problem is often reported to be part of a broader problem with rising hate group membership. This faulty correlation has been consistently reinforced by members of the news media, who tend to broadcast hate crimes statistics and shifts in hate group membership simultaneously.[33]

For example, in the aftermath of the shooting at the Holocaust Museum in Washington, D.C., in 2009, NBC Nightly News' Brian Williams explained, "Right now hate groups are at an all-time high. . . . This shooting today at the Holocaust Museum in Washington," Williams argued, "[is] the latest disturbing reminder that hate crimes are on the rise of late in this country, along with a number of groups that preach such messages."[34] Similarly, when ABC News aired a "Closer Look" segment titled "Hate Crimes" on May 2, 2007, Charles Gibson quoted Mark Potok, from the Southern Poverty Law Center, who claimed, "Since the year 2000, the number of hate groups is up 40 percent, from 602 to 844 today."[35] Such sentiments are not limited to network news broadcasts. In an editorial published in the New York Times, columnist Bob Herbert related the "increasing frequency and viciousness" of hate crimes to heightened hate group activity. Herbert argued, "Much of the hatred is fueled by the growing number of organized hate groups and the proliferation of Internet sites devoted to racism, anti-Semitism, homophobia, and other forms of intolerance."[36] As these examples show, when confronted with a particularly shocking hate crime, the mainstream news media seek out information about hate groups.

This assumed connection has led to faulty labeling practices and flawed policy objectives. The case of Bryan and David Freeman is illustrative. In 1995, the Freeman brothers, two neo-Nazi skinhead teenagers, murdered three members of their immediate family, including their sleeping younger brother. Their crime is clearly not, legally or logically, a "hate crime": parents and siblings are not included under anti-hate-crime laws' protections, and there are separate laws regarding child and spouse abuse. But, because the teenagers were poster children for the racist skinhead movement—two weeks before stabbing their sleeping parents and younger brother, the boys tattooed their foreheads with the phrases "Seig Heil" and "Berzerker"—the news media labeled their offense a hate crime. This inaccurate labeling underscores the significance of white power symbols in defining how hate crimes are perceived. In visibly claiming a white power identity, the Freeman brothers rewired how their crime was understood.

As the preceding examples underscore, hate groups play a decisive role within vernacular knowledge about hate crimes. However, as a theme, hate group membership rarely stands alone within portraits of prominent perpetrators. It is often the first detail included. But, as only one dimension within fuller portraits, hate group membership is later woven into more complex renderings. Prison culture, interracial gang activity, white power tattoos, mental health problems, and simply being a teenager are all enmeshed within depictions of hate crime perpetrators who belong to white supremacist organizations. Combined, these alleged character flaws produce a highly stigmatized white power identity.

John William King

John William King, one of the three men convicted of killing James Byrd Jr. in 1998, has been defined within the stigmatized terms described previously. Of the white-on-black crimes reported on since hate crime's invention, Byrd's grisly murder captured the nation's attention with unparalleled intensity. On June 7, 1998, John William King, twenty-three, Shawn Berry, twenty-three, and Lawrence Russell Brewer, thirty-two, stopped their truck under the pretense of offering James Byrd Jr., forty-nine, a lift home. In the one-sided fight that ensued, the three white men drank beer and smoked cigarettes while beating and kicking Byrd, slashing his throat, and spray painting his face. They then chained him to the back of their truck and drove down a three-mile stretch of road, maiming Byrd's body to the point of decapitation. King, Brewer, and Berry left Byrd's partial remains in Jasper's then racially segregated cemetery.[37]

Who did what the night of the crime remains unknown. Each of the accused pleaded not guilty. During their separate trials, each man's state assigned attorney posited theories that the other defendants were more actively involved in the beating and chaining. Their client had simply been in the wrong place, at the wrong time, with the wrong people. None of these defenses were successful. All three men were convicted of federal capital murder, including an additional kidnapping charge. Brewer and King received death sentences. Berry, whose defense managed to depict him as less obviously involved with organized white supremacy, escaped with a life sentence. As Texas had not yet passed anti-hate-crime legislation in 1998, none of the men was officially charged with committing a hate crime. This did not prevent the news media and politicians from labeling the offense a hate crime.

In the emotional turmoil that followed publicity of this case, everyone from President Clinton to NBA star Dennis Rodman was moved to words and action: President Clinton issued a strong, condemnatory public statement. Rodman volunteered to pay for Byrd's funeral. Even a south Texas Klavern of the Ku Klux Klan published a letter condemning the killing. For a number of arbitrary reasons, this case was a perfect storm for news coverage. Because the crime took place in 1998, a year when President Clinton was actively advocating for the passage of the Federal Hate Crime Prevention Act, politicians and news media producers were already primed to focus on the topic of hate crimes. Because the perpetrators chose to plead not guilty, very dramatic trials were staged. With the overwhelming evidence mounted against the perpetrators, the trials were more media event than judicial volley; prosecutors showed video footage of the blood-stained three-mile stretch of road and displayed the full length of chain as evidence before the jury. Because the crime happened in Texas, the very real possibility of the death penalty supplied added suspense to the sentencing phase of the trials. And, because the accused appeared to be unrepentantly guilty, watching their reckoning with the law was like imbibing a strong, restorative cocktail of retributive justice.

Due to the timing and publicity of King's offense, King became a—if not *the*—paradigmatic American hater. The *New York Times* alone ran 34 stories that included King's name. Combined, ABC, CBS, and NBC aired 122 stories dedicated to his case. The public and law enforcement officials first met King through his own self-destructive decision to write into local newspapers. In his letters, King claimed he was riding in the truck on the night of the crime, but had gotten out before the dragging took place.[38] Before sending in these letters, King had not been identified as a suspect. After he sent the letters, local authorities, with help from the FBI, investigated his property.

During the investigation, they found clothing and shoes stained with Byrd's body fluids; handwritten racist writings, including bylaws for a new white supremacist group King had named the Texas Rebel Soldier; and a KKK flag. After King was taken into custody, two young women he had corresponded with during his previous incarceration, two years prior, came forward with letters he had sent them filled with racist remarks. A KKK lighter discovered at the scene of the crime was also later identified as his. As these details emerged within coverage of the crime, King's public image began to take shape. The visibility of his affiliation with organized white supremacy and that affiliation's roots within the prison system factored heavily in how King was depicted.

As King's trial was held first, he became the central figure representing the crime to the widest audience. In the courtroom and in coverage of the case, prosecutors and the press rallied evidence of King's monstrousness, or simply asserted that King was evil. King was described variously as a "haunting monster" and as a "man without friends, without a future."[39] The state's prosecuting attorney, Guy James Gray, found one of King's motives to be "just being evil or Satanic."[40] Sharing this biblical interpretation, local Jasper resident Charlotte Hillard told *CBS Evening News'* Dan Rather that King was "the clearest picture of Satan that I think I've ever seen."[41] In the same summer when parents were already having to explain oral sex to their children thanks to President Clinton's Oval Office affair with Monica Lewinsky, Jim Axelrod informed *CBS Evening News'* audience that "murderer and thief [King] robbed a town full of children of their innocence."[42]

As the preceding quotations underscore, the task of vilifying King required minimal creativity.[43] And very little was expended. Despite the quantity of coverage dedicated to his crime and trial, descriptions of King himself tended to be flat. Instead of reporting on information about King's background, lifestyle, and character, reporters instead chose to speak with experts on extremism about racists in general or reiterate the same phrases and details from previously aired reports. The most reductive descriptions simply stated that King was "a white supremacist."[44] Offering a touch more detail, *NBC Nightly News'* Dawn Fratenglo described King as "an ex-convict who wears racist tattoos and allegedly belonged to white supremacist gangs while in prison."[45] CBS's Dan Rather depicted King as "a young man full of deep-seated anger and racial hate who wanted attention from the Ku Klux Klan."[46] *CBS This Morning's* early risers were told that King was an "ex-convict with ties to prison white supremacist groups."[47] These limited depictions touched on King's previous convictions, tattoos, and affiliations with white supremacist organizations.

More detailed profiles of King also tended to focus on his time in prison and his hate group membership. Significantly, discussions of King's prison experience imply that organized groups of racial and ethnic minorities trigger white supremacist activity. His two years of incarceration were described as a transformative period during which King changed from being a blue-collar dropout to being the "ultimate racist."[48] In a *New York Times* article titled "Unfathomable Crime, Unlikely Figure," Rick Bragg wrote that King was remembered as "a mannerly boy, quiet around grown-ups. His family was blue-collar Baptist. The only vice he had as a boy was snuff. He dropped out of school in 10th grade and did manual labor . . . he was just one of the sunburned young men who cruised town in ragged pickups with a six-pack. If he was overtly racist then, the people who remember him say they do not recall." Then King was incarcerated for robbery:

> [King] learned to hate in prison. Mr. King joined the Confederate Knights
> of America, a loosely organized prison gang for white supremacists. . . .
> Texas prisons have powerful black and Hispanic gangs, in particular one
> called the Mexican Mafia. They, and their white counterparts, espouse
> racial hatred. "The level of racism in prison is very high," said Mark Potok,
> a spokesman for the Southern Poverty Law Center. "The truth is, you may
> go in completely unracist and emerge ready to kill people who don't look
> like you."[49]

The narrative arc from unassuming, blue-collar kid to prison to virulent racist
was reiterated in other reports about King. These narratives implicitly argue
that learning to hate is something that occurs on the criminal margins, well
outside of tolerant mainstream America.

Reporting for *NBC Nightly News*, Tom Brokaw explained, "King's slide
from being a two-bit Texas thief to racist killer did not, by all accounts, begin
at home. King was raised the adopted son of blue-collar Baptists in the tall
pines of East Texas, on a racially mixed street in Jasper. And his father, Ronald King, has said there was no racial hate in their home, that their son's best
friend was actually a black child who lived a few houses down." After King
returned home from prison, his father was "stunned" to hear his son "spewing
the dogma of white supremacy":

UNIDENTIFIED WOMAN #1: He just came back somebody totally different.

UNIDENTIFIED WOMAN #2: You could tell he was different.

ANNOUNCER: A two-year transformation that shocked virtually everyone who
knew him. A cousin described a younger Bill King as quiet kid, really very
sweet. But he came out of this Texas prison, she said, really very big with
tattoos all over him, and none of them said "Mom." So, what happened
here, where two thirds of the inmates are minorities? In a letter he wrote
that he joined the Confederate Knights of America, a white supremacist group, most likely, experts say, to keep himself from being beaten or
raped. Once embraced and protected by the Aryan brotherhood, the larg-
est group, King became a devoted member, painting his body with symbols of racism, including a black man being hung. He became someone,
belonged to something, and he brought that back home.[50]

ABC News' Dina Temple-Raston, the reporter who spent the most one-on-
one time interviewing King during his trial, spoke in similar terms about the
significance of King's previous incarceration:

DINA TEMPLE-RASTON: Well, I mean, what the defense said, and certainly after
talking to a lot of Bill King's friends and people who knew him, prison
did something to him. Certainly there was a kernel of hate in him to

start with, because prison couldn't have done all of this. But certainly something happened to him in prison. And we talked a lot about his time in prison and how he was beaten up there and things like that. And the theory is that something much worse happened to him, but he's not willing to tell anyone.[51]

Notable across these narratives is the starting point: before being a racist killer, King was a small-time thief from a blue-collar background who dropped out of high school. These three different versions of King's prison conversion from "quiet kid" to "racist killer" emphasized the high percentage of minorities within Texas's prison population and the likelihood that King suffered some unspeakable abuse at the hands of minorities while in prison. Temple-Raston was the only reporter who insisted that King's racism, in an undeveloped "kernel," predated his time in prison.

If the prison system itself was being critiqued here, so too were the minority inmates who, it was hypothesized, forced King to associate with white racists in order to protect himself from assault and rape. In this framework, the prison's minority gangs actually produced the white racist killer. White racism was read as a reaction to aggressive anti-white sentiment, the assumption being that if minority inmates form coalitions, so too must white inmates. White racism becomes a natural, even necessary, defensive reaction to minority in-group organizing.

As King's case underscores, organized white supremacy, or hate groups, provide the visible signs that brand the figure of the hater. These loaded brands, with all their horror and cliché, make the embodiment of hatred legible. They are one hook upon which stigma can hang. But, white supremacy is not condemned in isolation. While not consistently central to public examinations of white hate groups, minority group organizations are still equally vulnerable to critique. The negative labels of supremacy and hatred do not meaningfully take power into account. White hate groups, African American prison gangs, and even noncriminal minority rights organizations can be cast in the same, undifferentiated negative light. The absence of power and inequality from the analysis of white hate groups versus minority organizations renders all identity politics projects equally vulnerable to the same accusations of failing to live up to the gold standard of not only color blindness, but also more comprehensively post-difference ideology.

MENTAL ILLNESS

The theme of mental illness also characterizes the crafted image of the American hater. Given the extreme nature of the hate crimes that garner news media and political attention, the people responsible for committing these hyper-violent crimes likely lack cognitive normalcy. In different terms, the nature of the coverage itself predetermines the nature of the publically exposed criminal. Within this universe of normalized extremes, hate crime perpetrators have been described as being "violently prone, mentally ill," as having "had a history of mental illness," and as being "emotionally disturbed, extremely paranoid, possibly even schizophrenic."[52] Of the top five most prominent hate crimes perpetrators, Buford O. Furrow Jr. had the most significant documented history of mental illness. An analysis of Furrow's public persona demonstrates how stereotypes about the mentally ill participate in both amplifying the demonization of haters and medicalizing bigoted belief systems.

Buford O. Furrow Jr.

On the morning of August 10, 1999, Buford O. Furrow Jr. opened fire at the North Valley Jewish Community Center in Granada Hills, California. He fired seventy bullets, nonfatally wounding seven people, including three children under the age of seven. Upon leaving the community center, he carjacked a Toyota and fatally shot a Filipino American postal worker. Furrow then successfully eluded a police dragnet overnight, during which time he shopped for a baseball hat and took a cab from Los Angeles to Las Vegas, only to turn himself in and confess the next morning.

In the months leading up to the shooting, Furrow was on probation for an incident nine months prior at the Fairfax Psychiatric Hospital. Furrow had gone to the hospital to check himself in, telling police at the time that he had been "having suicidal and homicidal thoughts." During the signing-in process, Furrow seems to have changed his mind and ended up waving a knife at the staff members. He was arrested, pleaded guilty, and served a five-and-a-half-month jail sentence followed by probation. Eighteen days after the shooting, in the hospital where Furrow's victims were treated, then California governor Gray Davis signed additional gun safety measures into law, including the most comprehensive ban on Saturday night specials, discounted, poorly made handguns most often associated with street crime.

Furrow's case received in-depth, sustained news media coverage from the crime scene through to his sentencing.[53] In the media frenzy surrounding the case, Furrow emerged as a paradigmatic hater, whose identity and life history could be used to teach a range of different moral, political, and cultural lessons. For those interested in the case's relevance to gun control laws, Furrow was described as "a deranged gunman" who "used a former police gun to murder" and who had assembled an arsenal stocked with "an Uzi submachine gun . . . an assault rifle, hand grenades and more than 5,000 rounds of ammunition."[54] For those interested in framing the case within debates over state policy on involuntary commitment, Furrow was "the latest example of a violently prone mentally ill man who snaps and attacks innocent people."[55] And for those who saw the case as a straightforward hate crime, Furrow was "a hard-core hater" and a "former Aryan Nations security guard."[56] Across these diverse characterizations, Furrow emerged as an amalgamation of different evils, weakness, and proclivities. A "heavily drinking mental patient with a passion for guns," Furrow was a natural-born folk demon.[57]

Aside from *Newsweek*'s Richard Turner, who opted out of the pomp of psychological profiling jargon and instead simply stated that Furrow was a "dysfunctional loser," most coverage of the crime succinctly described Furrow as a "white supremacist."[58] Over twenty separate articles and segments used the exact phrase "white supremacist Buford Furrow."[59] More detailed character sketches drew attention to Furrow's nasty temperament, affiliations with white supremacist organizations, previous criminality, and affinity for weaponry. The repetition of the words "loser" and "loner" throughout these descriptions unsubtly marks Furrow as both isolated and inferior. "What distinguishes Furrow from other stressed-out loners," argued *Newsweek*'s Andrew Murr, "is his avowed belief in the violent racism and anti-Semitism of the American Nazi movement."[60]

Widely distributed portraits emphasized that Furrow fit into a "familiar" profile. Reporting for *NBC Nightly News*, Fred Francis explained, "A man whose personality profile is familiar, unfortunately. He was a loner with a bad temper, racist views, and he did have ties to neo-Nazi organizations."[61] Peter Jennings stated for *Word News Tonight*'s viewers that "Buford Furrow also fits a profile that is familiar. A loner with racist views and a bad temper. He is a convicted criminal with a history of violence and weapons violations."[62] Notably, both Jennings and Francis argued that Furrow's profile was "familiar." The use of the word "familiar" situated what was a shockingly rare criminal act within a field of existing knowledge about the racist criminal mind. This kind of framing forwarded the faulty idea that bigots are obviously recognizable deviants. It also facilitated what would become a more bluntly stated critique of the state's mental health and criminal justice systems. The critique hinged on the state's perceived failure to recognize the full danger of Furrow's "familiar" type and, in ignoring these obvious signs, wrongly granted Furrow parole.

Reports printed in the *New York Times* and aired on NBC and ABC all emphasized similar aspects of Furrow's profile in ways that made the state's mental health and criminal justice professionals appear negligent. Ted Koppel, reporting for ABC's *Nightline*, explained that Furrow's "trail led to a mental institution, prison, and hate groups." He continued, "Buford Furrow was known to be a deeply troubled man who publicly proclaimed his racism and anti-Semitism and who had engaged in violent behavior before. He'd been identified. He'd been in and out of the justice system and in and out of the mental health system. Still, he was able to acquire massive quantities of weapons and ammunition."[63] Similarly, Timothy Egan reported in the *New York Times:* "What the experts saw was a man who twice slashed his arms so deeply that they required stitches, drank alcohol until he blacked out and espoused a deep hatred for anyone who is not white. . . . Mr. Furrow was an avowed racist who told a court last year that he fantasized about committing a mass killing."[64] These descriptions drew attention to Furrow's known mental health and alcohol problems, his explicit racism, and his history of institutionalization and incarceration. As both Koppel and Egan emphasized, the specifics of Furrow's derangement were "publically proclaimed," "identified," seen by "experts" and courts, and "espoused." Read together, these character sketches depict Furrow as an example of a known type and present his crime as something a properly punitive state could have prevented—if only a more preemptive penal logic had been effectively set in motion. This conservative tough-on-crime critique of the criminal justice system shows that certain kinds of institutional complaints can piggyback on hate crimes stories, just not ones that effectively illustrate the link between hate crimes and institutionalized forms of racism, homophobia, and xenophobia.

Furrow's public persona was further shaped by the two most widely circulated visual images of him. In one 1999 photograph, Furrow is being led, handcuffed, out of federal court in Las Vegas.[65] In the second photograph, taken in 1995, he is standing guard at an Aryan Nations outdoor event.[66] The photographs were taken four years apart, yet Furrow's expression appears unaffected by time, space, and context. He has the same bulky physique, the same slumped posture, the same dopey half smile, the same Hitler mustache, and the same receding pale orange hairline. In handcuffs, Furrow wore a yellow polo shirt, jeans, and a fleece vest. At the Aryan Nations event, he wore a custom-made royal blue uniform complete with an iron cross patch and leather bandolier. Despite differences in attire, Furrow's jovial expression in both pictures reads as decidedly inappropriate to anyone not sympathetic with the agenda of Aryan Nations. In handcuffs he is a criminal, in an Aryan Nations uniform he is a deviant. He appears mentally unwell in both.

These two images prompted the *New York Times'* editorial desk to describe Furrow as "something of a throwback, even among white supremacists." An outcast even among outcasts, "Mr. Furrow embodies the attributes, amounting nearly to a stereotype, that have made it all too tempting to regard white supremacy as a fading peripheral interruption within normal society."[67] The use of the word "tempting" implies that such easy assessments should be resisted. The full editorial warned readers that a younger, hipper racist right was gaining momentum. However, as the preceding examples have demonstrated, the vast majority of news media coverage of Furrow failed to resist the temptation to regard him as a stereotype, or as a "peripheral interruption."

Furthermore, the majority of law enforcement officials, politicians, newscasters, and journalists who spoke out against Furrow's crimes reveled in crafting this stereotype, or "profile," and perpetuating it in unproblematized terms. Images of Furrow earning a degree in engineering and working for Boeing, two aspects of his biography that might have changed how he was pigeonholed, were not widely publicized. Despite the *New York Times'* mild cautions, Furrow's case was predominately represented in terms that supported the inaccurate supposition that racism is a "fading peripheral interruption."

Discussion

Analyzing the figure of the hater and the content of his stigmatized identity reveals a cultural investment in marginalizing particular expressions of modern-day bigotry that play into, but also exceed, stereotypes about "poor white trash." The political stakes of this cultural investment are historically specific, ideologically inconsistent, and intimately related to the perpetuation of post-difference ideology. Before unpacking the hater's figurative powers, it is important to note that we know that the hater is a cultural construct because his defining characteristics, analyzed in the preceding sections, barely resemble empirically observed profiles of known hate crimes perpetrators.

Sociological and psychological studies of hate crimes perpetrators undermine stereotyped popular images of the hater. This body of research demonstrates that hate crimes perpetrators are, by and large, disturbingly conformist. As psychologist Edward Dunbar explains, "Less than five percent of hate crime perpetrators were identified as members of organized hate gangs or associations."[68] Similarly, the American Psychological Association has concluded that the majority of hate crimes perpetrators "do not fit the stereotype of the hate-filled extremist." Instead, "they are average young people who often do not see anything wrong with their behavior."[69] Along similar lines, it is worth reiterating that as the vast majority of all hate crimes recorded by the FBI in the Uniform Crime Report are minor offenses perpetrated against property, not against people. These crimes' perpetrators are not hardened, psychopathic murders, so much as they are petty vandals, macho teenagers, binge drinkers, and even college students.

Given these findings, the hater appears to be a clever news media construct whose amplified demonization both mirrors stereotypes about poor white trash and reflects overarching trends in the recent history of reporting on crime. In order to understand the significance of the hater within a society that actively seeks to define itself as both post-difference and perfectly tolerant, the intersecting processes of intra-white stereotyping and neoliberal constructions of crime are both essential. In essence, we find ourselves at an unlikely crossroads between whiteness studies and cultural criminology.

Recent work in the field of whiteness studies has made significant theoretical contributions to our understanding of intra-white stereotyping and its derogatory labels. In explaining how the terms "hillbilly," "redneck," and "white trash" function as racial markers, anthropologist John Hartigan Jr. argues that these degraded white identities become receptacles within which to dump the remainders of racism. "These are the figures whites use to delimit an attention to the subject of racism," Hartigan explains. "Consistently, these are the images and people whites turn to when they need to think about or are confronted with the reality of racism in this country." Hartigan further argues, "Part of what the epitaph white trash expresses is the general view held by whites that there are only a few extreme, dangerous whites who are really racist or violently misogynist, as opposed to recognizing that racism is an institutional problem pervading the nation and implicating all whites in its operation. In this naming operation, 'bad' whites perform as examples by which the charges of racism can be contained."[70] As these figures work against a broader recognition of racial and racist social forces, Hartigan suggests that recognizing "the important work these stereotypes perform in maintaining a prevailing image of whiteness as racially unmarked and removed from the blot of racism" is a critically important task.[71] Representations of haters offer one specific point of entry into this process of intra-white stereotyping and its embeddedness within post-difference thinking.

Fully comprehending the figure of the hater's cultural and political work, however, requires attention to how class-based stereotypes reach out into other stigmatized arenas, or perhaps more accurately seem to magnetically attract additional derision. Where whiteness studies has demonstrated that stereotyped images of the white underclass have been made to carry the stigma of contemporary racism, my research reveals a more multifaceted cultural construct being asked to do the same work of removal. While haters are certainly depicted as being "white trash," they are also the carriers of other modes of deviance: their criminality, flawed performances of masculinity, hate group membership, and mental illness all participate in making them a particularly virulent subspecies of "white trash." These representations perform tolerance through tough-on-crime rhetoric that is inflected with not only classism, but also stereotypes about masculinity, criminality, prison culture, and insanity and that expresses a deep-seated bias against identity politics. Instead of regarding each of these stereotypes and biases as separate, distinct traits, it seems more plausible that they potently enable each other. An underlying disregard for the contemporary challenges historically marginalized communities face bolsters the perception that punishing "white trash haters" will ultimately solve the hate crimes problem.

The stigmas and biases that have come to define the figure of the hater are best understood as nested within the historically specific political dynamics of the 1990s. The hater is simply one kind of extreme criminal figure within a menagerie of recently invented, similarly appalling figures, including the teenage superpredator and the Internet-based child pornographer. Scholarship from the fields of cultural and critical criminology, particularly the work of criminologists Vincent Sacca, David Surette, and Robert Reiner, has shown that since the late 1960s, representations of crime generally have become increasingly dichotomized between victims and perpetrators and increasingly skewed toward hyper-violent crimes. This body of scholarship demonstrates that before the mobilization of tough-on-crime politics and the institutionalization of a victim's rights agenda, news stories about crime were more attentive to perpetrators' perspectives. Since the late 1960s, representations of criminals became increasingly less sympathetic in ways that lent ideological validation to a host of neoliberal criminal justice policies, including harsh sentencing reforms, increased state funding for law enforcement, the privatization of the prison system, and the galloping expansion of the security industry.[72]

Examining how the mass media deal with crime, criminologist Martin Innes explains that the news media have come to "amplify" the demonization of perpetrators.[73] This relatively recent process of amplification tends to tread along familiar cultural pathways. As criminologist David Altheide argues, "Ideal type criminals are often members of despised and powerless groups in society."[74] The cultural construction of the hater falls within the purview of this overarching shift within representations of crime and criminals generally. Simply, the extreme terms used to describe haters are part and parcel of a broader news trend toward casting all criminals in an ever-more unfavorable light.

Haters, like other criminals, tend to enter into the public sphere only if they have committed extreme, violent offenses. Once they become objects of public fascination, they are depicted in ways that amplify their demonization. The hater stands at this crossroads between images of the criminal and images of the white underclass. By tapping into well-established neoliberal suppositions about both the white underclass and criminals, the hater has become the most prominent image of modern-day bigotry. In turn, the news media and politicians present the hater's public punishment, which includes both actual criminal proceedings and derogatory publicity, as an effective means of combating the hate crimes problem.

Conclusion

While haters are seemingly irredeemable figures, acknowledging the nasty stereotypes that underwrite their demonization is a necessary means of fully conceptualizing how intangible expressions of violence thwart our efforts to combat bigotry and promote tolerance. The cultural visibility afforded to the figure of the hater is harmful in and of itself. In knowing this figure we are less likely to accurately comprehend the reality of bias-motivated victimization in our everyday lives, or acknowledge the actionable seriousness of nonbodily expressions of bias-motivated harm. We are, however, encouraged to perpetuate familiar stereotypes about class, masculinity, mental health, and recidivism; to consume salacious narratives about racially divided prison gangs that show black and Latino violence spawning white racism; and to buy into the premise that a tough criminal justice system is needed. This process of stereotype affirmation does little good for the necessary, difficult task of mitigating the kinds of social harm experienced by members of historically marginalized groups. Ultimately, the fuss and drama surrounding this figure hint at a broader disenchantment with the project of promoting racial justice and civil rights.

CHAPTER 5

Hate Crime Victimhood and Post-Difference Citizenship

It is without question that articulations of victimization
have become an important cultural device that arguably
masks the problem of real victimization.

—Sandra Walklate, *Imagining the Victims of Crime*

ON JANUARY 16, 1992, the *New York Times* published an article titled "Young Bias-Attack Victim Tries to Laugh Off the Pain." Twelve-
year-old Bryan Figuero was the young victim. "On his way to school on
Monday morning," reported journalist Maria Newman, "[Figuero] was set
upon by several teen-agers who roughed him up and smeared his face with
white makeup." Figuero described being kicked and punched and feeling that
the menacing teenagers were "laughing and making fun of my culture." In
reporting on the crime, Newman caught up with Figuero, his mother, Diane,
and his best friend, eleven-year-old Ahmed. During the interview, Figuero
stated, "I wish we could all be the same color." In response, Figuero's mother
inquired, "And what color would that be?" "Maybe a little bit of orange,"
Figuero decided. Ahmed instead chose turquoise. Perhaps "a collage, like *Star
Trek*" would be the ideal universal skin color, guessed Figuero's mother. At
which point she joined the boys in "laughter."[1]

Moments like this matter to the cultural history of hate crimes because
they draw to the surface the often-submerged consequences of recognizing
hate crimes victims within a post-difference frame. In Figuero's case, being
targeted because of his "culture" sparked a psychological desire to eviscer-
ate visible differences in skin color. His wish that we could all be "the same
color" is itself a longing not for color blindness, but for the eradication of visible differences. The element of humor stems from the two boys' outlandish
choice of colors, orange and turquoise. Where the older teens used humor to
menacingly make Figuero the butt of their sadistic ethnic joking, Figuero used
humor recuperatively. For the two boys, this kind of joking can be read as a

plausible sign of their emotional triumph over trauma. At least this is how the *Times*' journalist perceived the situation.

But, the content of Figuero's longing—the wish for sameness—is a mark of our failure to combat bigotry and promote tolerance in ways that unconditionally acknowledge the role historic patterns of intergroup inequality continue to play in defining the contours of American life. Within the mainstream news media, hate crimes victims are depicted in terms that contribute to this failure. Members of historically marginalized groups gain access to victim status, not legally, but socially, on very limited cultural terrain. In detailing these boundaries, this chapter draws theoretical innovations from the fields of victimology, harm studies, hate crimes studies, and critical race studies into conversation with each other.[2] This intersection between fields helps further highlight the myriad ways in which cultural production is implicated in the social harm caused by hate crimes. But first, what is potentially harmful about the content of hate crime victims' mediated, public personas?

Much of the harm caused by images of hate crimes victims is the direct result of the news media and national political figures' conditional acknowledgment. During the peak years of hate crime news coverage in the late 1990s, only a select few victims, who met specific criteria, were granted sympathetic visibility. Now, with coverage of hate crimes waning, even fewer victims are recognized publically. Even the most widely recognized victims still find important aspects of their identities and histories "covered." The term "covering," as defined by sociologist Erving Goffman and applied more recently by legal theorist Kenji Yoshino, is used here to label the practice of toning down a disfavored identity trait in order to conform to social norms.[3] Within symbolic interaction theory, "covering" traditionally refers to adaptive behaviors utilized by individuals to downplay their own potentially stigmatizing attributes, such as wearing concealer over a birthmark or not discussing maternal responsibilities in a competitive work environment.

While Goffman uses the term to describe actions taken on the part of individuals to manage others' perceptions of them, a similar process can also be seen within more removed cultural contexts. I adapt the term "covering" to refer to a specific set of rhetorical tactics deployed by the mainstream news media in reports on hate crimes victims. In news segments and articles, cultural producers cover what they consider to be unfavorable aspects of hate crimes victims' identities, life histories, and political perspectives. This process of vicarious covering manages how audiences perceive and respond to these victims. It also reveals a great deal about what kinds of minority opinions and practices the mainstream deems unfavorable. For broad national audiences, the very substance of hate crimes victimhood is constructed through processes that cover differences and that cover the expression of political sentiments that make these differences meaningful. While heightening audience sympathy for these victims may appear compassionate, the kind of information that tends to be covered highlights how marginalized identity politics, racial justice, and civil rights work have become. An impossibly fine-grained cultural sieve separates out victims who do not vocally promote post-difference values.

Outside of legal contexts, hate crime victimhood is now contingent upon the victim's ability to perform "post-difference citizenship." As Evelyn Nakano Glenn insisted in her 2011 Presidential Address to the American Sociological Association, "Citizenship is not just a matter of formal legal status; it is a matter of *belonging*, which requires *recognition* by other members of the community."[4] Yet, when we are made aware of specific homosexual hate crimes victims, they are introduced in infantilized and desexualized terms. When we hear from specific victims of racially motivated hate crimes, they speak to us about the importance of color blindness. When we meet victims of anti-Arab and anti-Muslim hate crimes, they foreground their patriotic love of America. Each of these acts of vicarious covering can be understood as a performance of "post-difference citizenship." I define "post-difference citizenship" as the media process whereby members of historically marginalized groups and their allies are given access to public support by condoning post-difference ideology. Full citizenship rights to belonging and recognition are earned by disowning specific minority grievances.

The rhetorical tactics listed above demonstrate that hate crimes victims are defined in ways that nourish a post-difference worldview. By contributing to the robustness of post-difference thought, these representations undermine the relevance of contemporary civil rights struggles and bolster retributive criminal justice policies, which disproportionately punish members of racial and ethnic minority groups. Furthermore, these narratives revictimize actual hate crimes victims. By binding sympathy to specific acts of covering, the dominant cultural image of hate crimes victims actually does a disservice to real victims. "In our increasingly diverse society, all of us are outside the mainstream in some way," explains Yoshino, "nonetheless, being deemed mainstream is still often a necessity of social life."[5] Yoshino argues that countering the social compulsion to cover should be at the forefront of contemporary civil rights platforms because the ability to fully express even mutable differences is a fundamental, yet easily dismissed, human right. Compulsory covering can be understood as a pervasive form of alienating violence, especially when it is systematically practiced by the news media in depictions of members of historically marginalized groups. "The notion of alienating violence," explains sociologist Jamil Salmi, "refers to denying a person the right to psychological, emotional, cultural, or intellectual integrity."[6] Mainstream depictions of hate crimes victims are rife with alienating denials that reaffirm post-difference ideology. In sum, mainstream recognition, sympathy, and support are achieved at the expense of future victims' political integrity.

Who Speaks for Hate Crimes Victims?

One of the most common shared characteristics of prominent hate crimes victims is death: all of the most well-known hate crimes victims have been murdered. This focus on homicide results from the news media's preexisting tendency to normalize extreme cases, thus representing the issue of crime generally, and the issue of hate crimes more specifically, as shockingly violent. One consequence of this spectacularly morbid reporting trend is that victims' own self-representation is not part of how the problem comes to be known to the public outside of policing and advocacy circles. In place of self-representation, the public gets to know victims of hate crimes through information shared by law enforcement officials and actors within the criminal justice system and through the victim's friends, family members, and advocates. These more intimate associates of the victim have access to what can cynically be described as "grief capital." Social actors savvy enough to rally grief capital exert an, albeit limited, agency within media framing of their loved one's case, solicit vocal public support for legislative action, and apply public pressure during criminal proceedings.

A taught flirtation between these actors and the media develops over the life span of individual cases. The most adept grief capitalists speak on behalf of their victimized loved ones within legal, political, and cultural fields and are able to change the political content of their message. Over time, spokespeople for popular hate crimes victims can, if they so choose, revise their public message. Some of the most publicly visible spokespeople for hate crimes victims, including the families of both James Byrd Jr. and Matthew Shepard, underwent processes of radicalization. After verdicts were reached in each criminal trial, these spokespeople shifted from espousing a universal message about the tragedy of crime and began, in more partisan, progressive tones, to position Byrd and Shepard, respectively, as martyrs for African American and LGBT civil rights. This pattern suggests a tension between winning sympathy from the broadest possible audience, which translates into pressure for a harsh verdict during the trial phase of the crime's public life, and then creating an enduring cultural memory of the victim within particular social movement circles. However, once a victim has gained popularity, his or her spokespeople are not able to control fictive or journalistic reimaginings—the victim, as a known cultural figure, is subject to and subject of multiple, creative reinventions beyond his or her loved ones' preferred framing.

"MATT DID NOT FLAUNT HIS SEXUALITY": IMAGES OF VICTIMS OF HOMOPHOBIC AND SEXUAL-IDENTITY-BASED HATE CRIMES

No single hate crime victim has been subject to and the subject of more cultural visibility than Matthew Shepard.[7] As sexual orientation and gender identity are the two most contested categories within anti-hate-crime laws protections, Shepard's exceptional case is best understood as nested within a broader contest over visibility and victimhood. The debate over whether to include language pertaining to sexual orientation and gender identity within anti-hate-crime laws is an important backdrop to Shepard's visibility, as is the recent history of gay rights activism in the United States.

In the late 1980s and 1990s, at a time when LGBT communities were becoming increasingly vocal even as they continued to be persecuted, both politicizing and publicizing victims of sexual-orientation- and gender-identity-motivated hate crimes became tentatively possible. During this period, strong opposition from the religious right and from a vocal neoconservative "family values" platform confronted the increasingly well-mobilized gay rights movement. The legal status of sexual minorities was actively contested across the entire political spectrum. New patterns and practices of visibility were being met with firm denials of full citizenship. In popular culture, out gay and lesbian sitcom characters and celebrities were, for the first time, reaching mass audiences. Meanwhile, radical activists in Act Up and Queer Nation were staging acts of civil disobedience to raise awareness about the AIDS epidemic, anti-gay violence, and prejudice in the media. Despite this heightened visibility, even the most basic equal rights amendments securing nondiscrimination in employment and housing were running aground against staunch political opposition.[8]

While anti-hate-crime legislation generally enjoyed bipartisan support prior to the beginning of President George W. Bush's administration in 2001, the inclusion of sexual orientation and gender identity under the protected group membership categories was met with adamant resistance from conservative legislators at both state and federal levels. In order to avoid being perceived as supporting "the gay lifestyle" or affording "special" protections to homosexuals, the majority of states that passed anti-hate-crime laws in the 1990s chose to exclude the category of "sexual orientation" from their legislation. Of the twenty-two states that passed anti-hate-crime laws in the 1990s, only nine chose to include sexual orientation in their statutes and an additional five states found their amendments effectively blocked or revised to delete the phrase "sexual orientation."

The omission of sexual orientation from state-level anti-hate-crime legislation was not remedied on a federal level until 2009. By enacting the

Matthew Shepard and James Byrd, Jr. Hate Crimes Prevention Act of 2009 (HCPA) on October 22, 2009, President Barack Obama granted federal protection to victims of violent hate crimes motivated by sexual orientation and gender identity who had previously been excluded from state-level protection. In order to dodge opposition, the HCPA of 2009 was folded into the National Defense Authorization Act for Fiscal Year 2010.

Prior to the 2009 HCPA, legislators excluded the categories of sexual orientation and gender identity from anti-hate-crime laws despite the Justice Department's own findings. Research conducted by the Justice Department in 1990 found that homosexuals were a highly victimized population that was underserved, if not further victimized, by law enforcement officials. Resistance to evidence of homophobic victimization was particularly pervasive in Washington. The Justice Department suppressed its own initial exploratory report on law enforcement's ability to respond to bias-motivated crimes. The decision to suppress the report came immediately after news media outlets leaked the report's conclusion that "homosexuals are probably the most frequent victims of hate violence in America today."[9]

As gay and lesbian victims were being written out of the concept of hate crimes legally, the battleground for inclusion moved into hate crime's cultural and political life. In this contest for control over the meaning of hate crimes, and debate over whether homosexuals belonged under the concept's umbrella, the figure of the victim was singularly essential. But, the process of selecting an ideal-type homosexual, transgender, or transsexual victim—one who would appear both innocent and sympathetic to a mainstream audience— was problematic. The limited coverage of these victims focused largely on single, young, white gay males, the most prominent example being Matthew Shepard.[10]

More than any other single hate crime, Shepard's 1998 murder captured news media attention, activist energy, and political clout. Labeled a martyr for gay rights, Shepard was mourned in vigils nationwide, which attracted both adamant support and equally adamant protestation from the religious right. Shepard's death became a rallying call for a number of celebrities and the subject of multiple news specials. His death was lovingly commemorated by Ellen DeGeneres, Barbra Streisand, Melissa Etheridge, Elton John, the Tectonic Theater Project, and MTV, among others. Outside of Hollywood elites, a foundation exists in his honor and Lambda grants college scholarships to openly gay students in his name. Despite more contemporary anti-gay hate crime murders, Shepard remains the paradigmatic gay hate crime victim. The nuances of his mediated persona reveal a great deal about the fraught construction of homosexual hate crime victimhood in the news.

Aspects of Shepard's personality, life history, and physical comportment have all been rallied as character evidence in the court of public opinion. In shorter television news segments about the crime, Shepard was described as "the gentle young man from Wyoming" and as "the gay college student" with a "clean-cut image."[11] "Kind" and "polite" were the first two words that came to the mind of the bartender who served Shepard on the night he was killed. During a *20/20* broadcast hosted by Diane Sawyer, the bartender elaborated, "Very few people do you find in a bar that say, 'please,' say 'thank you' religiously. Matthew did that."[12] These short descriptions mildly amplify Shepard's claim to innocence by noting that he was open about his sexual orientation, productively engaged in higher education, in possession of a tidy personal appearance, and exceptionally well-mannered.

It is important to note at this point that Shepard, like the other most well-known hate crimes victims, is a murder victim. As such, Shepard is a mute cultural figure. In the inevitable absence of his own perspective, Shepard's parents were given voice to speak on his behalf. The news media's preference for heterosexual parents as spokespeople for victims of homophobic hate crimes, instead of lovers, friends, or members of the LGBT community, is a primary tactic in desexualizing and depoliticizing these victims' cultural memory.

Longer profiles of Shepard further magnify his innocence by erasing his history of consensual gay sex, by describing him in childlike terms, by highlighting his conformity to heterosexual norms of self-presentation, and by focusing attention on his role as loving son within a heterosexual family. Shepard tended to be remembered publically as a "sensitive child" and as "a young man with dreams." In reporting on Shepard's funeral for NBC's *Saturday Today*, Roger O'Neil paraphrased Dennis Shepard, Matthew Shepard's father, saying, "He made no mention of his son's homosexuality. . . . But, as the young boy's mother, Judy, sobbed, the father spoke not of hate, but his son's loving heart."[13] Similarly, during a *Dateline* news special dedicated to Shepard's case, Katie Couric noted, "Matt did not flaunt his sexuality."[14] "My son, Matthew paid a terrible price to open the eyes of all of us who live in Wyoming, the United States and the world," implored Dennis Shepard while delivering his victim impact statement. "You [the jury] may have prevented another family from losing a son or daughter."[15] Each of these statements focuses attention on Shepard's role as child within a heterosexual family. Despite being twenty-one years old at the time of this death, Shepard was still described as a "young boy."

Stories about Shepard being suspended in a state of perpetual immaturity were woven into subtle arguments about his claim to innocence. In the same *Dateline* special mentioned previously, Katie Couric interviewed Judy

Shepard, Matthew Shepard's mother. The interview cast Shepard in the role of winsome Peter Pan:

COURIC: The many ironies of Matt Shepard's star-crossed life are not lost on his parents, beginning with his physically small stature. When he died, he was little more than five-two and 105 pounds.... He was always sort of a scrappy little kid, wasn't he? A bit of a fighter?

MS. SHEPARD: Growing up, you know, the small size, to see everybody else grow up bigger than he was. He had braces when he was thirteen. Well, when he—when he died, he still had his braces on. Everything seemed to take longer for him.

COURIC: While he didn't excel at sports, he liked camping and fishing. And his parents say that from an early age, Matt was drawn to theater.[16]

The emphasis on Shepard's small physical build and delayed puberty work against narratives of the night of the crime, rallied by the defense, that cast Shepard in the role of sexual aggressor. In his mother's memory, directed by Couric's existing sense of the crime and of Shepard as an increasingly relevant cultural figure, Shepard's homosexuality was expressed through his interest in theater—not his interest in sex with other men. In this quotation, Shepard's gayness fit into existing stereotypes about male homosexuals being more theatrical than athletic. But he was not so gay as to forgo the masculine fun of fishing and camping. These examples illustrate that as Shepard became an iconic hate crime victim he aged backward from a college student out drinking to a stunted son being mourned by his spectacularly normal white middle-class parents.

Descriptions of Billy Jack Gaither mirror representations of Shepard. Gaither, like Shepard, was a comparatively prominent homosexual hate crimes victim. He was killed violently less than a year after Shepard, which was still well within the peak late 1990s period of hate crimes news coverage nationally. Like that of Shepard, Gaither's murder was reported on by numerous national news media outlets and became the subject of President Clinton's public condemnation. News media coverage of Shepard and Gaither emphasized their roles as good son and praised their nonflamboyant expression of homosexuality. Furthermore, each man's gayness was determined by nonsexual habits; where Shepard was described as being naturally drawn to theater, Gaither's home decorating skills were duly noted.[17] Gaither's choice to adorn his bedroom with pink curtains and *Gone With the Wind* memorabilia was a loaded detail within his perceived performance of suppressed homosexuality.

In-depth coverage of Gaither's case focused attention on his role within his parents' household. Numerous reports explained that the thirty-nine-year-old Gaither lived in his childhood home in order to provide care to his elderly parents. "Until the day two weeks ago when he was beaten to death and burned, Mr. Gaither lived with his disabled parents in their white clapboard house," reported David Firestone for the *New York Times.* "[Gaither] tended to their needs, cooking dinner, and cleaning up."[18] "Billy Jack Gaither was a devoted son," explained Jane Pauley during an NBC *Dateline* special, "he had a steady job, cared for his elderly parents, went to church."[19] "He was a real nice, loving boy," remembered one local woman during an interview with the *New York Times'* Kevin Sack, "good hearted."[20] Ruminating on his son's cultural memory, "Mr. Gaither said he hoped his son would not be remembered as a gay murder victim, but as 'one of the finest sons a man could want,'" reported the *Times.*[21]

Beyond his status as a devoted son, reports highlighted Gaither's wholesome lifestyle. Significantly, Gaither's decision to keep his sexual orientation private from his family was positively incorporated into stories about his being a good son and devout Christian. In an ABC *20/20* special dedicated to the case, John Quiñones reported that Gaither was a "deeply religious man who sang in the church choir, loved country music, and dancing, and just happened to be gay." One local woman interviewed for the same *20/20* special elaborated, "[Gaither] wasn't ashamed of who he was, but he wasn't flamboyant about it."[22] "A few friends knew that Billy Jack was very discreetly gay," explained journalists Daniel Pedersen and Arlyn Tobias Gajilan in a *Newsweek* article titled "A Quiet Man's Tragic Rendezvous with Hate."[23] Similarly, the *New York Times* explained that Gaither "never troubled his devoutly Baptist parents with the truth about his homosexuality."[24] The phrases "just happened," "very discreetly," and "never troubled" all underscore Gaither's decision to put his commitment to his parents over and above expressions of his sexual orientation.

A more detailed article on Gaither's family life further relates his role as good son with his choice to "not flaunt" his homosexuality. Reporting for the *Times,* David Firestone stated that Gaither's parents were unaware of their son's homosexuality:

> His parents swear they had no idea he was gay, and his father, Marion Gaither, is still half in denial, desperately pointing out that his son once had a girlfriend in Birmingham whom he almost married. Mr. Gaither's parents had barely absorbed the horror of his gruesome death before they were forced to learn the motive for his murder, and the secret life that he had led for so long. They knew him as the kindest of their four boys, the one who read his big illustrated Bible every night before going to bed, who never came home late on those rare occasions when he did go with friends to one of the local bars (all of them straight).

"If he was gay, he sure never showed it," his mother, Lois Gaither, said this morning. "He never flaunted himself as being gay or talked about it. And whether he was or not, it don't make me love him any less. He was my young'un," she added, in a kind of rueful acknowledgment of the truth. "Whatever he did, he never brought it home."[25]

This report depicts Gaither in childlike terms. He is remembered for being devout from a young age and for protecting his parents from his sexual orientation. The image of Gaither as a "young'un" reading an illustrated Bible nightly underscores a perverse, heteronormative cultural tendency on the part of mainstream news producers to idealize desexualized, infantilized homosexual victims of hate crimes.

In renderings of both Gaither and Shepard, the innate innocence of childhood is parlayed into a narrow, idealized image of victimhood. Despite being adults, both Shepard and Gaither were remembered primarily for their role as children within straight families. Read together, these narratives situate the problem of homophobic hate crimes within the parameters of heterosexual family life. In doing so, they distinguish between an essentialized, acceptable gay identity, which is characterized by mild effeminacy, and irredeemable homosexual sex. By reiterating that Shepard was drawn to theater from an early age and that Gaither used interior decorating as a creative outlet, these narratives reproduce stereotypes about gay men's artistic sensibilities. Ultimately, these reports amplify Shepard's and Gaither's claims to innocence by celebrating the fact that neither victim flaunted his sexuality. This particular image of homosexuality is a heteronormative fantasy that disallows LGBT anger, activism, and difference; the construct attaches public sympathy to an unpolitical, nonthreatening, easily recognizable version of what homosexuality might mean.

The tacit support for not "flaunting" that permeates these narratives affects which victims are and are not the subject of public recognition. National political figures and the national news media have yet to extend in-depth, individual attention to victims who are lesbians, bisexuals, queer people of color, intersexed people, people in long-term homosexual relationships, people who have a history of participation in gay and lesbian "lifestyle" activities and associations, or elderly homosexuals. These victims' sexuality and gender identities disrupt stereotypes and call attention to the intersectional nature of society's identity-based privileges and oppressions. As such, their experiences of victimization do not fit within existing news themes about hate crimes. This complex marginality means that these victims' plight remains largely invisible in the public sphere. Advocacy organizations, documentary and independent filmmakers, and a small handful of academics draw a more limited audience's attention to these victims. The most highly acclaimed example of this is the

1999 Academy Award–winning film *Boys Don't Cry*, which dramatized the circumstances leading up to the murder of transgendered man Brandon Teena.

Violence against transsexual, intersex, and transgender people, despite being one, if not *the*, most highly victimized population, is rarely afforded national attention, as in the exceptional, and graphically violent, murder cases of Brandon Teena, Gwen Araujo, and, more recently, Angie Zapata. Despite the tremendous violation suffered by Teena, Araujo, and Zapata, public debate over these cases equivocated between sympathy and blame. If extended, sympathy was doled out in stingy allotments. These victims' transgression of gender norms was read as discrediting. Their ability to achieve innocence was tarnished by their performance of gender (read as a lie), which mismatched their biological sex (read as truth). They were also embedded within narratives about desire and sex, where they were read as deceptively seductive. They were seen as both victimized and victimizing.

Reporting for the *Times*, Dan Frosch titled his story on Zapata "Death of Transgender Women Is Called a Hate Crime." As the title reveals, what was most notable about Zapata's killing was the fact that it was being "called" a hate crime. The article contains a biographic sketch of Zapata that juxtaposes her physical beauty—"her long hair, baby-smooth face and distinctive looks, Ms. Zapata cut a glamorous figure"—with details about her drug abuse, prostitution, and dishonesty. Unlike coverage of idealized, popular hate crimes victims such as Shepard and Gaither, coverage of Zapata emphasized her "troubled," "lonely" past and placed her as an active agent in her own social rejection. Her killing may have been labeled a hate crime, but she was not depicted as a fully sympathetic, fully innocent victim.[26]

The way in which Teena's, Araujo's, and Zapata's innocence was undermined by their gender identity and active sexuality begins to hint at the underlying cultural work involved with crafting the myths and images necessary to politicize certain, carefully chosen, victims of hate crimes. In the case of sexual-orientation- and sexual-identity-motivated hate crimes, being "innocent of sex" is perceived as a necessary determinant in being innocent of the crime. As literary scholar Beth Loffreda explained in her analysis of the Shepard case, "Matt was an innocent victim—of which there is no doubt—[that] doesn't mean that we need to see him as innocent of sex, of desire; but in the minds of many I spoke to . . . the latter seemed to taint the former."[27]

"I THOUGHT ALL THIS RACIAL STUFF WAS OVER WITH": VICTIMS OF RACIALLY MOTIVATED HATE CRIMES

Victims of racially motivated hate crimes are similarly forced to be innocent of race. When victims of these crimes, or these victims' surviving relatives, are given voice within the public sphere, they tend to speak in color-blind terms. Spokespeople for these victims perform innocence of racial difference in three ways. First, these spokespeople define racism as a problem history has solved, except in the case of a few criminally bigoted individuals. Second, they prioritize forgiveness over anger. Third, they empty skin pigmentation of social meaning. Racism's social saturation and institutional lodging are notably absent from these narratives, as is anything that could be perceived as Afrocentric assertiveness. When these victims' spokespeople connect their loss to struggles for civil rights, they do so through nonpolitical, religious terms that compare the victim's death to Christ's intentional sacrifice. Speakers who utilize these discursive tactics affirm the salience of post-difference ideology by distancing victims of racially motivated hate crimes from both contemporary racial issues and any trace of the Black Power movement's critique of white America.

Given the opportunity to speak to mainstream audiences, victims of racially motivated hate crimes define racism in two ways: In the first, the racism of slavery and the Jim Crow era is defined as an ugly chapter in America's past that the momentum of history has progressively resolved. Second, the racism that motivates modern-day hate crimes is defined as a much more limited problem that is perpetrated by criminal individuals and that can be effectively solved by law enforcement authorities and the criminal justice system. For example, after the hate crime murder of twenty-six-year-old J. R. Warren in 2001 in Grant Town, West Virginia, Warren's closest friend told Ted Koppel on ABC's *Nightline* that "J. R. was not killed because he came from a racist town. He was killed by two people who are part of an element which is not tolerant."[28] "Fighting back tears," Charlene Lovett, the mother of a fourteen-year-old hate crime murder victim, was quoted in the *New York Times* in 2007, saying, "I never thought something like this could happen here in L.A."[29] In each statement racism was perceived to be both an individual criminal problem and a surprise to black people.

Relatives of the most prominent racially motivated hate crime murder victim, James Byrd Jr., made similar public statements in the period leading up to the convictions of his three killers. After the convictions had been achieved and harsh sentences assigned, Byrd's relatives spoke out in more partisan political terms. Before the convictions, however, the Byrd family distanced themselves from contemporary antiracist activism. "[Rene Mullins, James Byrd's daughter] says she didn't experience racial bigotry growing up in Texas," reported Gwen Ifill for *NBC Nightly News*: "Ms. Mullins, 'I never encountered racial matters one-on-one, in person.'"[30] In a *CBS Morning News* interview with Jim Axelrod, titled "Daughter of James Byrd Says Jasper Does Not Have Racial Problems," Mullins explained, "This is the first time I've ever encountered any kind of racial tendencies. I am twenty-seven."[31] "You know, it's not the color that did it to my father," Mullins argued later in the broadcast, "it was three individuals."[32] By defining racism as a problem caused by criminal individuals, Mullins's statements model color blindness.

In a 1999 interview with *NBC Nightly News*, Jamie Byrd explained her emotional and intellectual response to her father's murder in similar terms. Listen for the echo of Rodney King's "Why can't we all just get along?":

Ms. BYRD: I know. It was just—I never would think anything would happen. I thought all this racial and all this stuff was over with, and I never did think anything like this would happen.

CURRY: How would you like—what—let me ask you this. After all that has happened, what do you come away with in terms of racism in America?

Ms. BYRD: Everyone needs to just come together and forget about black and white, and we're all the same inside. We have the same blood. And I just think it's—it's stupid to still have this in today's 1999, going on another century. I just do not think that we should still go on with this.

CURRY: You don't think this is a symptom of everything that's happening in the world . . .

Ms. BYRD: Mm-hmm.

CURRY: . . . but rather these particular people? Well, thank you. And I think, Jamie, that your father would have been very proud of your courage today.[33]

In this quotation, Jamie Byrd struggled to relate the experience of losing her father to the experience of "racism in America." She shifted, seemingly unprepared, between expressing frustrated surprise to advocating for color blindness. The message from her own words is somewhat hazy; she seems eager to assert her own lack of prejudice and her personal inexperience with white racism. But she was also issuing a wake-up call to "forget about" racial differences. Significantly, Curry distilled a more direct message from the teenager's misty conclusions. In Curry's paraphrasing, Byrd's murder was not reflective of society's racial problems or "a symptom of everything that's happening in the world." Instead, the killing was simply the sorry outcome of "these particular people's" deviant malady.

Beyond defining racism as an individualized criminal problem, those given voice to speak on behalf of racially motivated hate crime victims bask in forgiveness while shunning hatred. For example, after a Jamaican American tourist was abducted and set on fire in Tampa, Florida, in 1993, Milo Geyelin reported for the *Wall Street Journal* that the victimized tourist, Christopher Wilson, was "by all accounts remarkably devoid of hate."[34] "I have no hate for no one tonight," J. R. Warren's mother asserted.[35] Similarly, Rene Mullins stated on *CBS This Morning*, "There's no hate in me whether you're black, brown, blue, or pink."[36] Unless we are talking about *Sesame Street*, Mullins's cutesy insistence that she does not hate people who are "black, brown, blue, or pink" makes absurd the problem of skin color discrimination. Each of the statements listed above actively favors forgiveness over hatred. The rhetoric of forgiveness espoused by these predominantly female spokespeople for popular hate crimes victims subtly distances these speakers from more overtly masculine, activist, and militant African American voices. The refrains "there's no hate in me" and "I have no hate" can also be read as affirmations of Christian theology and rejections of Black Power.

Even victims of egregiously sadistic hate crimes have been publically quoted insisting on their lack of animosity. Roy Smith's disturbing case is illustrative. Over a period of several years in the early 1990s in Colorado, Roy Smith was the victim of severe racial harassment, which was ignored by local law enforcement agents. During the period of abuse, Smith had acid poured onto his clothing, had dynamite thrown into his home, was attacked repeatedly by a neighbor's dogs, was hit by a car, and was hung upside down, naked, inside his own home and threatened with castration. The police file documenting these assaults was labeled and filed under the name "Nigger Roy." "I have no hatred against none of them," explained Smith during an episode of *20/20* dedicated to his case, "anyone that I thought was my enemies. I don't hate any one of them. Hate ain't any good. It tears you apart, and only the hater loses."[37]

As these examples highlight, coverage of racially motivated hate crimes creates opportunities to further legitimize the post–civil rights era's dominant racial ideology: color blindness. Spokespeople for these victims model post-difference citizenship through the use of three rhetorical tactics. First, they relegate racism to the social margins and to the pages of history. Second, they occupy a moral high ground in a quality of forgiveness that transcends anger. Last, they conflate actual differences in skin pigmentation with imaginary colorations, thus masking the social significance of skin color. While these tactics influence how hate crimes are understood within public debates, their saturation is itself notable. Obvious truths do not usually require constant verbal reinforcement. The reiteration of these themes within news media coverage of anti–African American hate crimes unintentionally highlights the real possibility of alternate readings of these crimes' meaning and significance, which have been pointedly articulated by groups such as the NAACP and the New Black Panthers and by prominent figures, including the Reverend Al Sharpton and Louis Farrakhan.

The brutalized victim of racial violence has historically functioned as a powerful motif in the struggle for African American civil rights. The archetypal model was the fourteen-year-old lynching victim Emmett Till, who was murdered in Mississippi 1955. In accord with his mother's wishes, Till's corpse was shown to the public and photographed as an undeniable sign of racism's most visceral depravity. Images of Till's corpse were said to have "sparked" the movement.[38] In contrast, victims of racially motivated hate crimes tend to be represented in ways that undermine the relevance of contemporary civil rights work. When given voice to speak to mainstream audiences, spokespeople for these victims assuage white fears and white guilt. Victims of anti-Arab and anti-Muslim hate crimes are depicted in ways that similarly ameliorate fear and guilt and that further limit a sense of shared culpability.

"I Love America": Victims of Anti-Arab and Anti-Muslim Hate Crimes after September 11, 2001

In contrast to representations of homosexual and African American hate crimes victims, the rhetorical strategies used by the news media to depict anti-Arab and anti-Muslim hate crimes are less intimately sympathetic to victims and less directly punitive toward perpetrators. Considering the sheer number of stories about the rise in anti-Arab and anti-Muslim hate crimes in the wake of September 11, 2001, intuitively the victims and perpetrators of these crimes should have been included within the mainstream's purview. However, victims and perpetrators of these crimes remained largely anonymous. Victims tended to be buried in mathematically impersonal narratives about "rising rates" and "troubling trends."[39] Meanwhile, perpetrators of these crimes did not become objects of public disgust. No rituals of status degradation were performed during the public adjudication of these cases.

Anti-Arab and anti-Muslim hate crimes were verbally condoned. But, unlike Byrd's dragging or Shepard's beating, the motivation driving anti-Arab and anti-Muslim hate crimes seems to have been more comprehensible to mainstream audiences of news consumers. Politicians and newscasters spoke out against these crimes. But, they did not spend ink pondering "why" questions. The absence of individual anti-Arab and anti-Muslim hate crimes perpetrators and their victims from the public's gaze suggests that these criminals' actions, while reprehensible, were not unthinkable and that the victims of these crimes were difficult for mainstream American audiences to sympathize with.

The select few Arab American and Muslim American hate crimes victims whose stories received sympathetic publicity after 9/11 were hardworking, fully assimilated, nonradical, loyal American patriots. These victims achieved sympathy through mediated performances of patriotism, labor, and consumption. News coverage of hate crimes victims Balbir Singh Sodhi, Waqar Hasan, and Dean Hachem are illustrative. A few days after the 2001 terrorist attacks, Balbir Singh Sodhi was killed in Mesa, Arizona. He was an Indian Sikh who was wrongly perceived to be Muslim by his assailants. In an *NBC*

Today segment about the murder, Matt Lauer spoke with a friend of Sodhi's who explained, "He [Sodhi] called to his son in San Francisco, and he say, 'I want to go to New York to help those people to, you know, move those debris, all those things.' And he said, 'No, daddy, you can't do that. This is a professional people who does those kind of work.'" Lauer concluded by reporting that Sodhi, heeding his son's advice, instead, "went to his local Costco to buy American flags for the gas station he owned. And before leaving, donated all of the money in his pocket, $75, to a victim of September 11th fund. He was shot and killed less than an hour later."[40]

Descriptions of a Pakistani hate crime victim, Waqar Hasan, contain similar themes. Shortly after the 2001 terrorist attacks, Waqar Hasan was murdered in Texas, leaving his family vulnerable to deportation. Representative Rush Holt (D, NJ) took a personal interest in the case and drafted legislation to help the family members become U.S. citizens. Holt chose to advocate on behalf of the Hasan family because "they are working to make it in America. They're the kind of people we want in America." Mr. Hasan's widow, Durre Hasan, was also quoted publicly saying, "They [her neighbors] were very supportive and they came to my house and give me comfort. . . . It is easier to work in America as a women. Nobody cares if you are a man or a woman."[41] In this statement, Durre Hasan stakes a claim to post-difference citizenship by arguing that sex and gender differences no longer matter in the United States. This statement covers the role of sex and gender differences in the United States and then uses that covering as a launch pad to cheer American exceptionalism.

As these examples underscore, victims of anti-Arab and anti-Muslim hate crimes tend to receive public attention when they give voice to patriotic sentiments, when they are perceived to be hard workers, and when they take action against terrorism through consumerism and consumption. Overall, these reports draw attention to Arab and Muslim American voices that keep a positive, pro-American outlook. "While acts of kindness don't get as much attention," lamented ABC *World News Now*'s Dan Harris during a September 27, 2001, report on retaliatory hate crimes. "Muslims say, even in times of tension, they've found decency, not bigotry, is the norm."[42]

The *Wall Street Journal*'s detailed report on hate crime victim and small business owner Dean Hachem further highlights the cultural tendency to sympathize with pro-American victims of anti-Arab and anti-Muslim crimes. On March 13, 2002, the *Journal* published an article titled "How a Rumor Spread by Email Laid Low an Arab's Restaurant—It Said the Staff Was Jubilant on Sept. 11; Detroit Rallies Behind the Sheik, to No Avail." Written by journalist Jeffrey Zaslow, the article detailed how Internet slander, reportedly started by a local nurse, affected one Middle Eastern restaurant's reputation and decreased business by a noticeable 50 percent. Zaslow described the restaurant's patriotic decor ("American flags hang in the windows and around the dining room"), noted that Mr. Hachem had resided in the United States for over twenty-four years and had became an official U.S. citizen in 1985, and quoted Hachem stating, "I love America. . . . Until you've been on the other side of the world, you don't know to appreciate the United States, to kiss the ground here." In conclusion, the article related, "Mr. Hachem, meanwhile, has a request: If a nurse did see something in his restaurant, he wishes she would come to him. 'I'll ask her, "who did it?" If someone really cheered, he should be in jail, because down the road, he could hurt our country.'"[43] In this statement, Hachem explicitly marked his Americanness by modifying the term "country" with "our" and articulating emphatic support for preemptive criminal justice policies designed to combat terrorism.

Hachem's statements, read in conversation with the preceding examples, underscore the significance of expressed patriotism and antiterrorist sentiment in defining anti-Arab and anti-Muslim hate crime victims' claim to innocence. These victims' ability to achieve sympathy was contingent upon a particular performance of Americanness that was pro–government power, unwaveringly positive about the United States, especially when in direct comparison to their country of origin, and eager to define citizenship in terms of work and consumption—not political participation. The *Wall Street Journal* article's stated purpose was to expose the financial damage caused to Hachem's restaurant by the false accusation. Yet in reporting on this economic malice, the article labored to amplify Hachem's innocence by relating details about his citizenship status, patriotism, and support for preemptive counterterrorism policies. These are all details that fit into an overarching pattern of defining which victims of anti-Arab and anti-Muslim hate crimes deserve sympathy— all details that should arguably be irrelevant.

As these examples demonstrate, publically acknowledged victims of anti-Arab and anti-Muslim hate crimes were perceived to be patriotic workers, consumers, and members of assimilated families. Not only were they out heeding President George W. Bush's advice to shop the nation out of trauma, but they were buying American flags and donating to the New York relief effort. Despite the reported pervasiveness of anti-Arab sentiment during this moment in American history, which should have lent itself to substantive critiques, publically audible victims of anti-Arab and anti-Muslim hate crimes instead gave voice to a resoundingly pro–America message.

Cultural anthropologist Nazia Kazi argues that Islamophobia is matched by an equally powerful cultural process of Islamophilia, which celebrates representations of the "good" American Muslim. In her framework, stereotypes of Arab and Muslim Americans are binarily divided between "good" and "bad," with goodness being contingent upon assimilation through labor and consumption.[44] As the examples analyzed above highlight, the victims of anti-Arab and anti-Muslim hate crime whose stories were deemed newsworthy were all "good" Arabs. Akin to coverage of homosexual and African American hate crime victims, in this context "goodness," which is a stand-in for sympathetic, is defined as the abstention from political critique and the maintenance of a nonthreatening, passive posture toward state power.

VICTIMHOOD AND POST-DIFFERENCE CITIZENSHIP

The representational patterns described here have significant ramifications for understanding the relationship between post-difference ideology and the cultural construction of hate crimes victimhood. Where I have previously shown that representations of hate crimes legitimate a post-difference worldview, I now want to critically examine the social harm implicit within this cultural work. The conditional, exclusive process of recognizing who constitutes a sympathetic hate crime victim described in this chapter contributes to rendering victim status inaccessible to the majority of everyday hate crime victims—who show up at the scene of the crime and in life as politically complex, identity laden, visibly different, and perhaps even un-angelically miffed, unforgiving, or traumatized.

There is evidence to suggest that, as a society, we are miserly when it comes to empathizing with real hate crime victims. In a recent study of how young adults perceive hate crimes victims, sociologists Kellina M. Craig and Craig R. Waldo found that "less than a quarter of all respondents indicated that victims of hate crimes were innocent." In essence, the overwhelming majority of young adults surveyed felt that the victims of hate crimes were implicated in the harm done to them. Similarly, sociologist Christopher J. Lyons argues that hate crimes victims are confronted by a wall of "social ambivalence" that is as likely to produce stigma and blame as it is to grant sympathy. For gay and lesbian victims in particular, Lyons states that "sympathy is not evident."[45]

Within victimology's professional lexicon, ascribing blame to victims is termed "victim precipitation." Victim precipitation theory, while intellectually outdated, clearly still has a mass audience when it comes to defining the problem of hate crimes. As hate crimes are nested within social contexts, the prevalence of skeptical and accusatory attitudes toward victims troublingly suggests that these victims cope with their experiences within a less than compassionate environment. Indifference, if not outright blame, is the norm. When victims are not perceived to be innocent, the way in which their colleagues, coworkers, classmates, and family members respond to them may worsen their experiences of victimization. This process has been labeled "secondary victimization" and has been identified as one of the central harms caused by hate crimes. As Craig and Waldo explain, "Responses to victims may represent a secondary form of victimization either through ignorance or rejection."[46] The representational patterns I detail in this chapter are part of the overarching cultural and political context within which this kind of ignorance and rejection retains legitimacy.

While secondary victimization may seem like an unintended consequence of unwieldy social and cultural forces, new research within the field of critical victimology posits a more functional relationship between how victimhood is defined and the state. Critical victimologists Basia Spalek and Sandra Walklate highlight the complex interplay between the state's investment in defining citizenship and its interest in controlling access to victim status. In elaborating the way in which our society has come to individualize emotion, Spalek argues, "Victims' needs have been framed and used by the government . . . victims' emotional reactions to the harms that they have experienced have been translated into individual need using the discourses of consumerism and active citizenship."[47] "Victimhood has become elided with citizenship," Walklate explains. "In this sense victimhood is the status whereby the state, through increasingly subtle and not so subtle global and local processes is reasserting its power over citizenship." Walklate then insists, "Victimhood is harnessed as a source of oppression in the interests of the increasingly diverse and hegemonic (capitalist) state."[48]

Spalek's and Walklate's assessments of the state's role in eliding victimhood with consumptive citizenship have disturbing implications for the way in which hate crime victims are represented. The state and the news media's involvement in designating who counts as a legitimate hate crime victim can be read, in part, as a process of renegotiating the terms through which members of historically marginalized groups are able to make demands on the state. This renegotiation relegates more radical demands for structural, institutional changes to the margins while prioritizing criminological reforms. As this chapter has underscored, the differences that distinguish members of historically marginalized groups, including both their collective memories of oppression, exclusion, and trauma and their awareness of the harm wrought by contemporary biases, are reduced to meaningless liabilities within mainstream representations of hate crimes victimization. Given this post-difference premise, these representations implicitly question the logic of valuing these differences as sources of positive identification and as sites for mobilizing group action.

CONCLUSION

Crime is a layered, largely invisible social experience that filters out into the public sphere through media processes and political discourses. The vast majority of all criminal activity, including hate crimes, will never be accessible for any kind of spectatorship. Cultural context is particularly crucial to understanding hate crimes victimization because it delimits the terms of recognition and denial, which have been perpetually under negotiation since the concept was invented. Culture mediates between access to emotional resources and the denial of these same resources. Put differently, the experience of hate crimes victimization is lived both within the actual moment of the crime and again in the broader world of community, citizenship, and everyday life. The narratives about prominent victims discussed here offer one specific site where members of historically marginalized groups and their allies are given the opportunity to make status claims, not through assertions of systemic vulnerability, but through a resounding dismissal of identity politics. These kinds of depictions indirectly validate indifference toward real hate crimes victims and legitimate an individualized, criminal-justice-based approach to the problem.

The mainstream news media and national political speech is now part of the hate crimes problem. These powerful institutions are both culpable for the social harm attributed to hate crimes. This subtle social harm crystallizes within stories about hate crimes that portend to condemn these violations while also invalidating, misrepresenting, and belittling contemporary efforts to promote social justice for historically marginalized groups. Yet, culture is still a necessary front for anti-hate-crime activism and advocacy. Performance artists, poets, documentary filmmakers, and other cultural producers, many of whom come from within historically marginalized communities, can and have taken up the challenge of telling hate crimes stories in ways that productively rethink the nature of the problem and that imagine new ways of responding to these crimes in everyday life. These sometimes-gruesome, sometimes-playful pieces promisingly buck dominant trends and suggest that new cultural practices have real potential to change how we comprehend and cope with hate crimes. In the epilogue, I introduce a few of these exceptional works and consider how the knowledge of subaltern cultural producers can contribute to efforts to resist hate crimes victimization.

CHAPER 6

Epilogue

CHALLENGING HATE CRIMES ON A CULTURAL FRONT

All too often our culture indulges in an entirely putative mentality towards those who are defined as different (something that is even more painfully evident in the general public indifference to the brutalizing impact of "law and order" initiatives and prison expansion in the United States). We seem to have largely lost the capacity for empathy, for imaging ourselves (or our circumstances) as different from who we are (or what they are). This identification can never be complete—we can never claim to fully inhabit the other's subject position; but we can imagine it, and this imagination, this approximation, can radically alter our sense of who we are. It can become the basis for communication and understanding across differences of race, sexuality, ethnicity, and so on.

—Grant H. Kester, *Conversation Pieces*

IN 2005, ARTIST MARY COBLE stripped down to the plainest white underwear ever manufactured and stoically endured twelve straight hours of inkless tattooing. The ordeal, or more judiciously "endurance performance," titled *Note to Self*, was staged in Washington, D.C., at Conner Contemporary Art, a gallery that focuses on conceptual art in nontraditional media. Prior to the performance, Coble immersed herself in research on victims of homophobic hate crimes. From her findings, Coble compiled a list of over four hundred victims' names, each of which she would tattoo on her body, and developed an analysis of the connection between individual hate crime victims and the broader role homophobia plays in shaping social and material relations in the United States. As her blood pulsed out of each fresh marking, an assistant dutifully pressed a clean piece of watercolor paper against the wound. Each new print transfigured the tattoo needle's damage into what

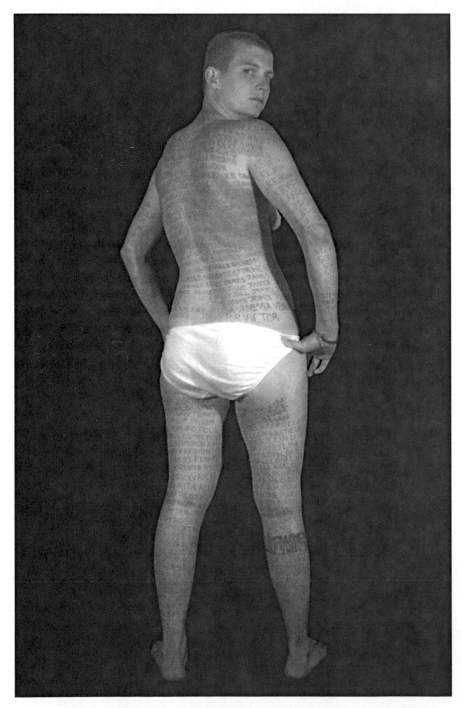

Figure E.1 *Untitled 1* (from *Note to Self*). Reproduced with permission of Mary Coble.

Coble describes as an "opportunity for a visceral reaction and reflection on the mental and physical violence that hate crimes enact on individuals and communities."[1] The performance symbolically co-opted hate crime perpetrators' strategy of carving slurs into their victims' bodies. Coble allowed her audience to witness the pain of bigoted branding and to think about its disturbing meaning in a space that was designed for dialogue. The long list of names was intended to produce a different effect from an individual memorial. Coble explained that she wanted "people to see a compilation of names, not to individually mourn, but to understand the broader scope."[2]

Coble's work invents visibility that then allows for reflection on pain that is usually hidden. The visceral presence of harm that her work enacts makes people uncomfortable. In a photograph taken at the end of the performance, Coble stands with her back to the camera, exposing her canvas. She looks back over her shoulder with an expression that is hard to decipher, but is certainly not nostalgic: Her intense direct eye contact is decidedly non-elegiac. It might well be angry.

Erin Davies's Volkswagen Beetle also makes people uncomfortable. On April 18, 2007, the Volkswagen Beetle of art education graduate student Erin Davies was assaulted with graffiti. A passerby noticed her car's rainbow sticker and sloppily scrawled the insults "fAg" and "U R gay" on the car's windows and body. Needing the transportation, Davies drove the tagged car to school and parked on campus. To her surprise, there was an outpouring of public response. People demanded that the car be moved, left notes on her windshield, and tried to talk her into removing her pride sticker.

Davies found herself in the middle of a strange new kind of public debate. Homophobes and hate crime victims alike shared more of their experiences and perspectives than Davies could possibly have predicted. The outpouring inspired Davies to leave the tags intact. Dubbing the car the "Fagbug," Davies drove the crime scene across the country for fifty-eight days, documenting her interactions on the road in a film of the same name. Davies's strategy is one of unflagging friendliness. She can and does talk to everyone. Even homophobes.

Davies describes her risky road trip as an act of "externalization" aimed at inspiring "important exchanges." An out lesbian prior to the hate crime, she explains that she let the car further out her in order to incite reaction and conversation: "A person's first response to something like that is to remove it and not be confronted, not to see it and erase the shame in it. That makes it so there's no unified experience. People feel they are the only one and live with that shame in the dark. I did the opposite. I externalized it rather than internalize it and by doing that other stories came to me." Davies's decision to "externalize" the hate crime committed against her raises unsettling questions: If victims consistently "externalized" these kinds of crimes, would homophobic,

Figure E.2 Katherine Wright, *Davies Jumping*, 2008. Reproduced with permission of
Katherine Wright.

racist, sexist, and xenophobic slurs be a familiar part of the American visual
landscape? Would trips to the grocery store or evening strolls with the dog be
littered with defamatory graffiti, much the way some American middle school
hallways ring with phrases like "no homo," "that's gay," and "nigga"? While
the Fagbug now reads as an interesting anomaly, if similar graffiti were left on
cars, garage doors, houses, and, as Coble's work painfully reminds us, victims'
skin, how might we think differently about and respond differently to bias-
motivated harm?

Beyond any aesthetic qualities, what fascinates me most about Coble's
and Davies's very different projects is their shared interest in changing how
hate crimes are perceived and responded to. In the first chapter, I asked the
following question: Is our collective cultural imagination capable of depicting contemporary modes of bigotry in a way that is accurate enough to allow
for informed action? If pressed to answer this question based solely on the
evidence I analyzed in the previous chapters, I would have to say no. My
study does not invite optimism. Our culture, however, is not composed solely
of corporate news networks, legislative debates, and presidential speeches.
Unlike the representations that I have been critiquing thus far, projects like
Davies's Fagbug and Coble's *Note to Self* aim at interaction, at exchange, at

conversation, at revelation. Cultural producers hailing from outside the mainstream have successfully created works that not only contextualize and historicize the problem but also highlight the real psychological costs that even micro-level, everyday acts of bias-motivated victimization exact on members of historically marginalized groups. In detailing the context and history behind individual hate crimes, these artist/activists underscore the impossibility of ever understanding these incidents without reference points beyond the crime scene and courtroom.

DIALOGIC ART PRACTICES AND SUBJECTIVE METHODS

In order to assess these alternative ways of addressing the problem, I have had to break from the previous chapters' structured methodology. I believe this shift is necessary because resisting bigotry on a cultural front requires opposition to the clichés and stereotypes that work against our ability to conceptualize other people's experiences of social harm. In order to find sources that do this kind of counterconventional cultural work, I had to enter a far less organized field of evidence and tap into a different mode of analysis. This epilogue focuses on a smaller pool of richer evidence that demands in-depth, close reading, opposed to systematic counting and coding.

The select few sources that take center stage in this epilogue were chosen from among many other wonderful antibias projects because they explicitly and intentionally challenge audiences to rethink the nature of hate crimes victimization. These are works that focus on hate crimes in meaningful contexts. In doing this work, they unmask the social forces that are all too often missing from the mainstream.

On a more personal level, I was drawn to these sources also because each makes me feel something beyond the melodrama and cliché served up by the mainstream and these emotional stirrings seem to be worth lingering over; these are feelings that help me reconceptualize the harm caused by hate crimes, past the superimposed flatness of crime-and-punishment narratives and into the nuances of human sociology, history, and psychology. Susan Sontag would point out, though, that "having an emotion is not the same thing as having an understanding, and neither is the same thing as taking action."[3] Yet, attunement to emotional nuance still seems to proffer a useful counterweight to the mainstream's overwrought, overdramatized, and paradoxically emotionless handling of hate crimes.

My interest in these works has been further informed by a line of conversation happening on the margins of art criticism. This conversation, whose most vocal participant is critic Grant Kester, focuses on the novel political and interpersonal possibilities introduced by collaborative, conversational art practices that merge activism, social work, and art production. Labeled varyingly as relational aesthetics, social practice, community-based art, and dialogical art, this highly differentiated body of work seeks to bind "new forms of intersubjective experience with social or political activism."[4] Such linkages, Kester tells us, grow out of avant-garde traditions that were informed by an Enlightenment era wish for emancipatory aesthetics.

As Kester notes, a range of Enlightenment era writings associate aesthetic experience with "a potentially utopian capacity for exchange and communication." At its best, this kind of work utilizes techniques traditionally associated with community organizing, such as the facilitation of ongoing, directed conversations within a politically salient community, to stimulate active listening, spark intersubjective vulnerability, and inspire empathetic insights and identifications.[5] Art critic Shannon Jackson suggests that this work finds ways to place "the possibility of death and the possibility of intimacy into the same space."[6] Poet, essayist, and art critic Maggie Nelson observes that this work is "most always predicated on the desire to lessen the amount of cruelty and miscommunication in the world."[7] Idealistically, practitioners in this field and their participants draw on Kant's "radical promise" that the aesthetic can provoke the "calculating and defensive individual" toward openness, receptivity, experimentation, and self-transformation.[8]

While skeptical, I too am deeply interested in the utopian potential of culture. Like Kester and Jackson, I too have sought out work that in my estimation has the potential to "help us speak beyond the limits of fixed identities, official discourse, and the perceived inevitability of partisan political conflict."[9] But, Kester warns against overreaching. Even while celebrating the richness of this emergent international trend, Kester is quick to offer this caution: "Not all conflicts can be resolved by free and open exchange because not all conflicts are the result of a failure among a given set of interlocutors to fully 'understand' or empathize with each other."[10] Even the most brilliantly conceived and masterfully executed dialogic art event will be better equipped to challenge individually held suppositions than to undo overarching systems of stratification. Such happenings may trigger shifts in individual perception, but are unlikely to unwind the workings of material power.

Given these pragmatic limitations, I value the work described here to the extent that it is able to pose open-ended questions that then provide a frame for critical reflection on the nature of hate crimes as historically rooted and socially embedded events. No one work or act can undo structural inequality, although it is fascinating to see projects, such as the national Occupy Movement that arose in September 2011 to protest economic inequality, that try. With reference to the hate crimes problem, these works succeed when and if they are able to unmask how structural inequalities and histories of antiminority oppression activate contemporary, subtle interpersonal harms. My rumination focuses on revelatory moments that attempt to communicate about the nature of bias-motivated harm across boundaries of interpersonal difference. What ultimately gets shared across these divides draws us back into distinctions between objective versus subjective violence and primary versus secondary victimization.

Repoliticizing Hate Crimes

Acclaimed American poet Mark Doty's prize-winning poem, "Charlie Howard's Descent," Whitney Dow and Marco Williams's documentary *Two Towns of Jasper*, and Christine Choy and Renee Tajina's Oscar-nominated documentary *Who Killed Vincent Chin?* layer revelation upon revelation. While I am strongly in favor of publicizing hate crimes as a problem primarily composed of low-level offenses, these three pieces demonstrate that it is possible to retain a focus on murder while still illuminating the interconnectivity of individual hate crimes and histories of minority exclusion, marginalization, and exploitation. To the extent that the hate crimes problem is in fact partly rooted in miscommunication and a subsequent withholding of empathy, and to the extent that the accuracy of works such as these energizes new modes of protest, then each work underscores the tantalizing potential for counterdiscursive practices to repoliticize hate crimes in ways that are relevant to the future of civil rights in the United States.

In "Charlie Howard's Descent," Mark Doty eloquently relates the story of a hate crime murder as an extension of a life lived in the ever-present company of homophobia. Doty's poem is based on the true story of Charlie O. Howard, who on July 7, 1984, was killed at the age of twenty-three by three boys between the ages of fifteen and seventeen. The teenagers threw Howard off of a bridge into the Kenduckeag Stream in Bangor, Maine. Unable to swim, he drowned. On July 13, 1984, the *Boston Globe*'s Michael Kranish reported that the teenagers had "bragged afterwards to a friend that they 'jumped a fag,' 'beat him up,' 'and threw him into the stream.'"[11] As part of a plea bargain arrangement, the three assailants pled guilty to a reduced charge of manslaughter. One was released after serving two years. The others served only twenty-two months.[12]

Doty begins his poem with the scene of Howard falling: "Between the bridge and the river / He falls through / a huge portion of night; / it is not as if falling / is something new. Over and over / he slipped into the gulf / between what he knew and how / he was known." The word "fall" takes on a double meaning. Doty connects the fall that occasioned Howard's death with the multitude of daily "falls" commissioned by the difficult space between how Howard perceived himself and how he was perceived by others—the classic experience of living with an unmanageable stigma.

Doty continues,

> What others wanted
> opened like an abyss: the laughing
> stock-clerks at the grocery, women
> at the luncheonette amused by his gestures
> What could he do, live
> with one hand tied
> behind his back? So he began to fall
> into the star-faced section
> of night between trestle
> and the later, because he could not meet
> a little town's demands,
> and his earrings shone and his wrists
> were as limp as they were.

In this passage, Doty questions Howard's life chances and life choices. The impossible choice between self-expression and self-denial lies at the core of Doty's question: Howard can either be himself and "fall" or live a life impaired by others' suffocating demands. For Doty, this is clearly not a choice at all so much as an incitement to "fall" with flair.

In the next passage, Doty begins to imagine Howard's life from different angles. "I imagine he took the insults in/and made of them a place to live." By selecting the word "imagine" Doty deferentially acknowledges the absence of Howard's own voice. As distant witness to Howard's death, Doty is left to speculate, to imagine—partial and imperfect ways of knowing, at best. But, as Kester writes, imagination is perhaps the best and only way of accessing an honest empathy. Doty continues by further developing his sense of how bias-motivated insults can be "made into" the instruments of survival:

> we learn to use the names
> because they are there,
> familiar furniture: *faggot*
> was the bed he slept in, hard
> and white, but simple somehow,
> *queer* something sharp
> but finally useful, a tool,
> all the jokes a chair,
> stiff-backed to keep the spine straight,
> a table, a lamp.

The metaphor Doty develops in these lines underscores a sense of utilitarian survival. By selecting the personal pronoun "we," Doty draws Howard's individual life experiences into a broader experience of sexual difference. When Doty states "we learn" he refers to the untenable process of being a homosexual socialized into a heterosexual society. From Doty's perspective, undergoing this process of socialization requires the individual to grasp moments of fulfillment from within homophobia's regime.

Having transformed insults into the tools of life, Doty's imagined Howard is then prepared, without morbidity, for his own violent death. At this point, the poem turns and splits. Howard begins to appear in spectacular Christ-like forms. "And because / he's fallen for twenty-three years," states Doty, "despite whatever awkwardness / his flailing arms and legs assume / he is beautiful / and like any good diver / has only an edge of fear / he transforms into grace." As homophobia was transformed into everyday furnishings earlier in the poem, the reader is now prepared for yet another transformative leap in which Doty rewrites the chaos of Howard's final fall into a moment of sheer divinity.

By adding another turn, Doty complicates his own authorial authority and Howard's voice:

> Or else he is not afraid,
> and in this way climbs back
> up the ladder of his fall,
> out of the river into the arms
> of the three teenage boys
> who hurled him from the edge—really boys now, afraid,
> their fathers' cars shivering behind them,
> headlights on—and tells them
> it's all right, that he knows
> they didn't believe him
> when he said he couldn't swim,
> and blesses his killers
> in the way that only the dead
> can afford to forgive.

These final stanzas offer an antidote to mainstream depictions of hate crime murders. As Doty has already established the pervasive intrusion of homophobia in Howard's life, he is able to conceive of quite a different relationship between victim and perpetrator.

Doty instructs his reader to reconceive of the relationship among masculinity, gay bashing, and bravery. In wearing earrings that "shone" and letting his wrists be "as limp as they were," Howard displays bravery by refusing to cover his homosexuality and in doing so draws to the surface increasingly menacing forms of homophobia. For Doty, Howard's outward presentation of homosexuality manifests the best qualities associated with masculinity, namely the bravery that rewards a strong sense of self. Meanwhile, the attempt of the "boys" to prove their adult masculinity by assaulting Howard only accentuates their own immaturity. Gay bashing renders them childish and afraid. Doty's sensitive description of the three killers highlights their youth, their vulnerability, and their normalcy. Too young to poses their own means of transportation, the killers are literally carried by their fathers' cars to the scene of the crime. The same cars cast a quivering light on their actions. The image Doty evokes of the scene of the crime suggests a hovering parental presence.

The nature of forgiveness Doty allows and disallows is remarkable. Only Howard can afford to forgive. Doty allows for the possibility that the crime may have been an accident, and that Howard, as a divine figure capable of resurrection, would fearlessly, compassionately forgive his own killers for their brutal mistake. All this Doty presents explicitly as his own fantasy, his own reimagining. And even in this space of infinite grace, the victim alone possesses a legitimate right to forgiveness. Society is not only still culpable, but also positioned as an illegitimate source of adjudication.

In many ways the conclusion to Doty's poem mirrors mainstream representations of idealized hate crimes victimhood. Like James Byrd Jr.'s color-blind daughters or the resolutely patriotic victims of anti-Arab and anti-Muslim hate crimes after 9/11, Howard comes to fully embody forgiveness. What distinguishes between the quality of forgiveness in Doty's work and the quality of forgiveness celebrated in the mainstream news media is the content of the narrative that precedes it. The angle of redemption widens. Howard's act of forgiveness is predicated within Doty's poem on an acknowledgment of the damaging role homophobia played throughout Howard's life. The boys' criminal actions arise in the poem as yet another act within an ongoing sequence of degradations. The boys themselves are pathetic bit players on homophobia's grand stage. If Howard forgives the boys it is only because their actions stem from social conformity, rather than individual malice.

The poem leaves questions of blame, of just punishment, and of forgiveness unresolved. In insisting that these questions remain adrift, Doty's work complicates the notion of getting "tough" on hate. But in invalidating one means of combating hate crimes, Doty breathes a renewed political energy into other modes of resistance: in muddling the ethics of the murder itself, Doty forces us to reconsider the subtexts and contexts within which homophobia does most of its everyday damage.

Much like "Charlie Howard's Descent," the documentary films *Two Towns of Jasper* and *Who Killed Vincent Chin?* both take prominent hate crimes murder cases as points of departure. *Two Towns of Jasper* documents the small eastern Texas town of Jasper as it endures the three contiguous trials of James Byrd Jr.'s murderers. As the title *Who Killed Vincent Chin?* suggests, the film tells the story of Chin's murder in a way that expands the circle of culpability beyond the two convicted killers themselves. Both films amass evidence of racial and ethnic disunity, specifically ontological differences in how histories of oppression and violence are either activated or negated within contemporary hate crimes discourse. They also provide evidence of the magnitude of suffering caused by hate crimes to both those who care about the victim and those who care about the perpetrator; evidence of how both overtly racist and color-blind racist minds work; evidence of how personal transformations in racial ideology happen or, more often, fail to happen; evidence of anger, resentment, agency, and activism from within historically marginalized communities; and evidence of a yearning for unity that is at times provocatively sincere and at other times performative and repulsively hollow. One of the most striking ironies these films capture is how communities, despite sharing the desire for reconciliation, are prevented from engaging in honest dialogue about the real scope and underlying causes of conflict, a containment strategy that makes sense only from the color-blind racist's vantage point.

To produce *Two Towns of Jasper*, filmmakers Whitney Dow and Marco Williams lived and shot footage in Jasper, Texas, from January through December 1999, during which time the three men accused of the murder of James Byrd Jr. were being tried. Dow led an all-white crew who filmed the town's white residents and Williams worked with an all-black crew to film the town's African American residents. This approach enabled Dow and Williams to enter into private, segregated spaces, often the only sites for accessing honest talk about race. In these sheltered social enclaves, Williams and Dow were able to witness what Williams describes as a "magnification of difference," which, while not an explicit aspiration of Choy and Tajina's film, is certainly one implication of it as well.

In his original introduction, which was first aired on PBS's *Point of View*, Williams explained that the film aimed at documenting both racial divisions and individual transformations: "It is a film about an incident that magnifies difference and what people do when they feel threatened by difference." While this seems action-oriented, the film actually captures rifts in perception, rhetoric, memory, and emotion. Choy and Tajina capture similar rifts by presenting in-depth interviews from a range of perspectives, including the killer's; by showing media footage from American television news alongside footage from Asian networks also covering the case; and by tracking the Asian American civil rights movement that condemned the lenient sentences Chin's killers received, alongside white rejection of said movement.

Two Towns of Jasper's underlying directorial project is revealed immediately by an opening that pairs two scenes that look carefully at the same strange object from two different perspectives. The object—a mysterious brown streak on a backcountry road, whose three-mile length makes it even more mysterious—is, in fact, the trace of James Byrd's body, as that body met and met again the friction of the road propelled by the momentum of Shawn Berry's moving truck. The film's first shot peers out of a windshield onto the surface of this same vacant, tree-lined stretch of road. The elusive brown smudge meanders back and forth across the pavement much like the elegant skid marks engraved by teenagers joyriding down empty rural roads. Both marks evidence a confluence of deviance and expertise.

The stain is, at first glance and without any context, hard for Jasper's white sheriff Billy Rowles to place. In the film's opening shot, Rowles explains his thought process at the very beginning of the investigation. From under the expansive brim of his white cowboy hat, Rowles states, "[I] knew it was a black man that was dead, hopin' that it was a black man who killed him. But it didn't turn out that way." One the other hand, the two African American morticians who retrieved Byrd's body were more certain about what the stain was and what it signified.

The film's second shot again traces the surface of the road. This time, the two morticians, both members of the Coleman family, accompany our witnessing. Leaning against the side of his hearse, Rodney Coleman explains that he knew immediately that he was looking at a "blood trail": "Right away we knew, or I felt, and I told my father at the time, I said Daddy, they, some white people, did it. Just had that gut feeling that it was race related." Where Rowles was "hopin'" the murder was not race related, the Colemans "just knew" that it was. The initial perception of the crime was informed by the racialized subject position of the viewer, which was in turn, as we see in the rest of the film, informed by said viewer's memory of the history of race relations and civil rights in Jasper.

Where *Two Towns* shows the divide between the African American and white communities in Jasper, *Who Killed Vincent Chin?* highlights similar divisions between Detroit's white and Chinese American residents. For Helen Zia, one of the most active civil rights advocates to mobilize Detroit's Asian American community in the wake of the murder, Chin's death crystallized a consensus. "The one thing that has pulled together, through sheer concern, all Asian Americans in this country and brought press and so forth from overseas and concern from overseas," explains Zia, "is the belief that Vincent Chin would be alive today if he were not Asian and there is no question about that in any of our minds." As Zia implies, the very idea that Chin might have been killed for nonbiased reasons seems ridiculously naïve, if not willfully ignorant.

Yet, the convicted killer, Ronald Ebens, and his friends adamantly deny the possibility of a bias motivation in the killing and object to the notion that Detroit's social fabric is infused with anti-Asian sentiment. "He is not guilty of doing this because of racial animus or racial feelings or racial bias or racial prejudice," claims one of the killer's friends, "it so happens the person he was involved with was Chinese." Another friend of the killer admits to not knowing much about the facts of the case yet insists that it was "an accident." Ebens, the same man who confessed to beating Chin's brains onto a McDonald's parking lot with only a baseball bat in hand, protests that he "never had anything against anybody." "I'm no racist," avers Ebens toward the beginning of the documentary, "I've never been a racist." His direct eye contact with the camera suggests that Ebens believes his own statement.

By including white interpretations that directly conflict with Asian American and African American interpretations of each crime, both documentaries externalize a host of profound differences in perception. Beyond simply noting these divisions, both films also rigorously document how these divides are premised on differences in historical memory: the minority communities in both films remember past injustices with ringing clarity, whereas white residents are at a loss to recount any past acts of prejudice and are thus unable to comprehend the contemporary legacy of these historic patterns of oppression. Professor of African American studies Lawrence Jackson defines this predicament as "that element of the past that we do not share." As Ebens complained, "They [the news media and Asian American civil rights activists] used it [Vincent Chin's murder] to promote their alleged plight in this country, which I am not aware of that they have a plight."

Like Ebens, Jasper's white residents are oblivious to their town's racist past and to the experience of African Americans in the wake of Byrd's murder. As Father Ron, one of Jasper's white ministers, explained, he decided to organize an interracial prayer gathering because local African Americans, not whites, felt healing was needed: "The white community has made an effort to make eye contact, to be more concerned. The white community feels that we have to do that because a tragedy happened in the black community and the black community feels that healing needs to take place, that it is necessary. I think white people do sometimes need to bend over backwards because they are feeling something that we are not feeling." Disturbingly, Father Ron describes the efforts of the white community, which up until that point had constituted little more than brief expressions of concern, as "bending over backwards." But he is right to note a gap in felt emotion over the killing.

Another, less diplomatic, white resident of Jasper reminisced fondly about using the word "nigger" freely during his childhood. At a regular gathering of the "Bubbas in Training" breakfast club, he expressed heartfelt confusion over why the town's racial lexicon had changed since the civil rights era. "I don't remember them [African Americans] taking it personal," he mused, "maybe they did and didn't say anything." What stands out in the reactions of both Detroit's and Jasper's white residents is the appalling degree of obliviousness. On film, they seem honestly perplexed, almost humorously out of touch. Of course none of this is funny to the people who were called "nigger," who vividly remember past racial murders that were followed by enforced silence instead of prosecution, and who struggled for civil rights while living only to be buried in a racially segregated cemetery.[13]

In contrast to the willful ignorance of Detroit's and Jasper's white residents, the Asian American and African American communities' long historical memory of bias-motivated victimization is well documented in both films. Through oral histories as well as home video footage, baby photographs, and other memorabilia, Choy and Tajina carefully reconstruct how pervasive anti-Asian sentiment affected everyday life for Detroit's Asian American community as it attempted to assimilate. In one difficult scene, Vincent Chin's mother, Lily Chin, describes the kind of xenophobic abuse she and her husband suffered when she first arrived in Detroit: "I got off the boat during the first month of the lunar calendar of 1948. We lived and worked in a basement laundry. But when the neighborhood kids saw us in the basement they made ugly faces. They stuck out their tongues and made as if to slit our throats. . . . We went to see a baseball game. But when people saw Chinese sitting there they kicked us and cursed us. I never went back." From one limited perspective, Lily Chin's memory of mocking threats and public derision has little or nothing to do with her son's eventual murder. But her memories provide a necessary backdrop to her son's death. They offer a window through which to better view the killing in context, a window that explodes simple notions of individual culpability. By including stories that reveal an extended history of marginalization and lurking violence, Choy and Tajina place Chin's singular murder into a broader social landscape of systemic, institutional, symbolic, and everyday anti-Asian violence in Detroit that shapes how that community continues to understand the crime. Even if Chin had survived, the community would still be justified in feeling unsafe and underserved. Williams and Dow document similar feelings of vulnerability, trauma, and rage in Jasper's African American community that are grounded in that community's long historical memory of white racism. As one African American resident explained, learning about the details of Byrd's murder was "more punishment for the heart."

Doty's, Williams and Dow's, and Choy and Tajina's distinct projects parse out lines of meaningful difference between objective and subjective violence and primary versus secondary victimization. If the projects are read as directives, it is possible to discern a particular call to action, or a particular line of intervention, to address secondary victimization, rather than striving fruitlessly to prevent murder. Much of what these three works accomplish in terms of helping to reconceptualize the hate crimes problem is premised on carefully crafted moves between revealing ontological divisions (between minority/majority and victim/perpetrator) and humanizing these same divisions. All three works make visible underlying differences in worldview at the exact moment that these differences are explained in wider historical, social, political, and economic context.

Both films also rely on the skillful navigation of relationships between the filmmakers and their participants over an extended period of time, a process and commitment Kester praises with the label "durational." The quality of access each film enjoys within the community it seeks to represent is monumental: Williams and Dow and Choy and Tajina successfully gain access to people who are willing to express unpopular views on race and ethnicity. They then allow these people to speak with snapping honesty on film. The brilliance of including bigoted perspectives is not that they shock our delicate sensibilities, although they may, but that they indirectly validate how members of historically marginalized groups who live in these communities define the problem at hand. Underlying safety issues and legacies of trauma, often hidden or ignored, become visible.

By giving voice to publicly unacceptable views and by shedding light on private experiences of victimization, these films simultaneously validate minority narratives and open up a space, similar to the space Coble's and Davies's works also activate, for reflection on the nature of the hate crimes problem. The films' revelations are messy in comparison to the law-and-order narratives favored by news producers and politicians. These works problematize the notion of culpability. They raise unanswerable questions about how harm is perpetrated and experienced. They do not solve or combat anything. But the very retreat from false sense making is itself a productive starting point for future anti-hate-crime action. In witnessing each of these works, we can adapt our anti-hate-crime efforts toward making secondary victimization and objective violence visible and thus open to critique.

INVENTING EMPATHY

"Today more than ever," claim sociologists Michael Omi and Howard Winant, "opposing racism requires that we notice race, not ignore it, that we afford it the recognition it deserves and the subtlety it embodies."[14] The publicity surrounding certain shockingly violent hate crimes presents a near perfect example of what happens if the second half of Omi and Winant's sentence goes unread: We end up trying to oppose bigotry from within our culture's uncontested biases. Our attempts at recognition are ultimately remiss, because the depth of our willingness to witness harm across lines of difference is insufficient. As senior editor at the *Atlantic*, Ta-Nehisi Coates, argues, the "basic extension of empathy is one of the greatest barriers in understanding race in this country. I do not mean a soft, flattering, hand-holding empathy. I mean a muscular empathy rooted in curiosity."[15] I do not agree that empathy must be scrubbed of any (feminine?) traces of tenderness in order to do its work. But I appreciate Coates's bigger point about curiosity and its resonance with the epigraph from Kester, who prioritizes an empathy empowered by imagination.

The works this epilogue explores also reveal a significant empathy deficit, which primed curiosity and imagination would help undercut. They also highlight the value of finding new ways to tell hate crimes stories, ways that transcend the now standard clichés and stereotypes. This kind of reinvention can help audiences better understand the nature of social harm. For some people, this may mean stepping away from the phrase "hate crimes" altogether. If met with a firm commitment to finding new ways to recognize and then address bias-motivated social harms, an abandonment of the phrase itself may be one of the only ways to transcend the narrow rhetorical framing of the issue, especially considering the increasingly offensive, dysfunctional, and conservative nature of the national debate.

However, there are three important points to be made about the context within which recognition might be made possible. First, our very desire for progress beyond bigotry works against its recognition. Second, our popular culture has its own stakes in reproducing the denial of bigotry. Third, the closer we look into the "facts" of severely violent hate crimes, the more likely we are to find ourselves adrift in mystery. "The more progress a society has made in denouncing racism as a social and political evil, the more vehemently its continued existence is denied," argues legal scholar Dimitrina Petrova. "Ironically, the denial of racism is a product of the progress of the struggle against it."[16] Petrova highlights the tension between the success of past civil rights movements and the present normative climate these achievements have created for contemporary antibias work. Fraught and fortuitous, progress is itself now an impediment to acknowledging the potency of contemporary bigotry.

What critical criminologist Simon Pemberton defines as "symbolic machinery" further camouflages the social harm wrought by depoliticized depictions of hate crimes. In his work on moral indifference, Pemberton argues that popular culture tends to promote indifference and create bystand-ers to harm: "There are compelling reasons to envisage a theory of denial as part of a theoretical continuum with indifference because the notion of denial allows analysis of the symbolic machinery required by capitalist society to ensure indifference to harm."[17] From Pemberton's and Petrova's perspectives, accurately apprehending the hate crimes problem is blocked by both the success of previous civil rights movements and the entire heft and sway of capitalist cultural production.

Beyond these ideological and material impediments to recognition, the appallingly violent hate crimes that have tended to garner national attention often devolve into unknowable mysteries under the scrutiny of serious investigation. Let me be clear: bias motivation is no more challenging to ascertain in a legal context than any other kind of legitimately recognized criminal intent. Conservative critiques of anti-hate-crime laws on the basis that these laws unfairly police non-politically-correct beliefs are out of step with the underlying design of our criminal justice system, which is finely tuned to account for intention in many criminal contexts. That said, the works this epilogue has focused on depict hate crime murders as fundamentally unknowable. The closer these works take us to the original crimes, the more the assumed or superimposed meanings of these crimes evaporate. The facts lose their explanatory power. We are left with tragedies that cannot be accounted for or dismissed through the accumulation of more facts.

These material, political, psychological, and epistemological conditions are real. They play an active role in limiting the likelihood of recognizing bias-motivated social harm. But they are more real for some members of American society than for others. As the works detailed in this epilogue underscore, many members of historically marginalized groups have no problem remembering past oppressions. Informed members of these communities continue to feel the traumatic legacy of long histories of bias-motivated violence. They cannot help but be aware of the cumulative effect of past prejudices and can identify contemporary acts of bias-motivated harm, even on a microlevel.

Perhaps we may come to consider the fundamental mystery of hate crimes murders as a gift. These crimes' elusiveness could productively prod us to seek meaning from the living, who will likely direct our attention to that which we can remedy. We do not need to heroically prevent hate crimes murders; instead we can find ways to refuse to participate in secondary victimization. The curiosity that fuels a "muscular empathy" might just require strong ears. In listening, the stakes shift. We are no longer simply bystanders alongside the Other's grief. As Kester's epigraph states, in order to learn how to communicate about social harm across the boundaries of difference, we have to be open to "radically altering our sense of who we are." That radical alteration is unlikely to flatter our patriotism. But it too is an American dream.

Appendix: Methods and Sources

I ARRIVED AT THIS book's claims by employing a transdisciplinary research process that integrated methods from history, sociology, American studies, and cultural studies. During this process, archival, news media, and legislative sources were gathered. Specifically, I examined internal memos from the Clinton administration and the Anti-Defamation League (ADL); conducted personal interviews with the initial architects of anti-hate-crime legislation, with the top administrator of MTV's anti-hate-crime campaign, with the current legislative director at the ADL, and with several artist/activists; and sifted through legislative hearings, anti-hate-crime legislation, newspaper and news magazine articles, and transcripts of television news broadcasts. Working inductively, I systematically coded, analyzed, and interpreted all of the archival, legislative, and news media sources, as well as the personal interviews and unarchived documents first to get a feel for underlying themes and a second time to further discover nuances within these themes.

As the news media analysis is the hub of the entire study, I worked with particular rigor in coding these sources. I conducted a systematically coded two-part discourse analysis of every article from the *New York Times'* section A, *Newsweek*, and the *Wall Street Journal* and of transcripts from ABC, NBC, and CBS News that include the exact phrase "hate crime(s)" and are also labeled by LexisNexis under the topic heading "hate crime(s)." While earlier sources were consulted in putting together the etymology and social history, the dates of the principal study range from December 1986, when the *New York Times* first printed the phrase "hate crimes," to May 2010. The sources studied were selected because they reached the widest audience of mainstream U.S. news consumers during the period of study and because they are word searchable on LexisNexis, except for the *Wall Street Journal*.

I printed out a total of 1,037 stories in hard copy, organized them chronologically by source in binders, and color coded them for type of crime committed, main characters, themes, and content details. I began by noting both dominant and outlying themes. Early on in this iterative process, I identified perpetrators, victims, and the nation as central characters. Armed with these observations, I retraced my steps within the sources listed above and within the wider source base. During this second round of coding, I marked every story that contained a detailed description of a hate crimes perpetrator, victim, or the nation and then observed patterns across and within this more discrete source base.

There are three main limitations to this approach. First, it fails to consider news sources with wide audiences that hail from a particular political position, including the powerhouse network Fox News. Second, on the opposite end of the heft spectrum, it also misses smaller-scale advocacy groups and their publications. The first and concluding chapters partially address this oversight. Third, it does not account for shifts in patterns of news consumption over the period studied. From the late 1980s through 2012, the traditional news networks studied, namely ABC, NBC, and CBS, lost viewers to the Internet and cable news networks with round-the-clock coverage, particularly CNN and the blogosphere. Disenchanted younger viewers flocked to comedy news reviews, like *The Daily Show* and *The Colbert Report*.

Given these omissions, future research on the cultural politics of hate crimes could fruitfully focus on sources that are self-consciously outside the mainstream, that broadcast via cable stations, or that publish online. A more diverse source base would likely offer a range of alternative perspectives on the problem. A comparison between liberal and conservative voices would be particularly fascinating and would likely dredge up greater inconsistencies between depictions of the problem than my study is capable of accounting for. In sum, what this study is able to conclude about mainstream cultural politics is achieved at the expense of delving into the nuances of less well publicized, more politically charged representations of the problem.

NOTES

CHAPTER 1   INTRODUCTION

1. The "FBI Uniform Crime Report Hate Crime Statistics for 2008," which is based on data from the Federal Bureau of Investigation's Uniform Crime Report, shows that the single most frequently reported hate crime is "damage/destruction/vandalism" committed against property. See http://www2.fbi.gov/ucr/hc2008/ (accessed June 29, 2013).
2. Martin A. Berger, *Seeing Through Race: A Reinterpretation of Civil Rights Photography* (Berkeley: University of California Press, 2011).
3. Randall Kennedy, *The Persistence of the Color Line: Racial Politics and the Obama Presidency* (New York: Pantheon Books, 2011).
4. These scholars include Barbara Perry, Mark Hamm, Benjamin Bowling, Kathleen Blee, Colin Flint, Jeannine Bell, Jack Levin, Jack McDevitt, Donald Green, Edward Dunbar, Gregory M. Herek, Kevin Berrill, Christopher Lyons, Martha Minow, Frederick M. Lawrence, Valerie Jenness, Ryken Grattet, James Jacobs, Kimberly Potter, Dimitrina Petrova, Sandra Walklate, and Rini Sumarto.
5. Karen Franklin, "Psychosocial Motivations of Hate Crime Perpetrators: Implications for Prevention and Policy" (paper, congressional briefing co-sponsored by the American Psychological Association and the Society for the Psychological Study of Social Issues, Washington, DC, November, 1997).
6. Jeannine Bell, *Policing Hatred: Law Enforcement, Civil Rights, and Hate Crime* (New York: New York University Press, 2002).
7. For a brief discussion of the etymology of "hate crimes," see Donald P. Green, Laurence H. McFalls, and Jennifer K. Smith, "Hate Crime: An Emergent Research Agenda," *Annual Review of Sociology* 27 (2001): 480.
8. James B. Jacobs and Kimberly Potter, *Hate Crimes: Criminal Law and Identity Politics* (Oxford: Oxford University Press, 1998), 4; Barbara Perry, "Where Do We Go from Here? Researching Hate Crime," *Internet Journal of Criminology* (2003): 2, http://www.internetjournalofcriminology.com/Where%20Do%20We%20Go%20From%20Here.%20Researching%20Hate%20Crime.pdf.
9. *Oxford English Dictionary Online* (January 2, 2010), http://www.oed.com.
10. "Urges Law on Hate Crimes," *Chicago Daily Defender*, April 5, 1960.
11. Victoria Irwin, "Race Tensions Surface in New York," *Christian Science Monitor*, December 23, 1986; Scott Bronstein, "Laws to Curb Bias Attacks Weighed," *New York Times*, March 2, 1987.
12. Irwin, "Race Tensions Surface in New York."
13. Linda Greenhouse, "Consequential Cases Are Likely to Test the Supreme Court's New Majority," *New York Times*, October 7, 1991.
14. David M. Raim, former Anti-Defamation League attorney, interview by Clara S. Lewis, Washington, DC, April 9, 2008.

15. Frederick M. Lawrence, interview by Clara S. Lewis, Washington, DC, 2008.
16. Barry Glassner, *The Culture of Fear: Why Americans Are Afraid of the Wrong Things* (New York: Basic Books, 1999), 29.
17. For more on the history and political implications of the war on crime, see David Garland, *The Culture of Control: Crime and Social Order in Contemporary Society* (Chicago: University of Chicago Press, 2001); Robert Reiner, *Law and Order: An Honest Citizen's Guide to Crime and Control* (Cambridge: Polity, 2007); Jonathan Simon, *Governing through Crime: How the War on Crime Transformed American Democracy and Created a Culture of Fear* (New York: Oxford University Press, 2007).
18. Jacobs and Potter, *Hate Crimes*, 5.
19. "Public Attitudes towards Crime and Criminal Justice-Related Topics, 105: Table 2.1," in *106 Sourcebook of Criminal Justice Statistics* (Washington, DC: Bureau of Justice Statistics, Office of Justice Programs, 2003).
20. "Attitudes towards Important Issues for the Government to Address, Table 2.2," in *106 Sourcebook of Criminal Justice Statistics*.
21. Memorandum from Ed Goeas and Dave Sackett to *United States News and World Report*, "Re: Key Findings from United States News IV National Survey," May 28, 1993, Clinton Presidential Library Archives, Domestic Policy Council, Bruce Reed, Crime [OA 8412], box 71, folder 10.
22. Ibid.
23. Memorandum from Rahm Emanuel to Leon Panetta, "Subject: Crime Planning," September 15, 1994, Clinton Presidential Library Archives, Domestic Policy Council, Bruce Reed, Crime [OA 101826], box 79, folder 7.
24. Ibid.
25. Ibid.
26. Letter from the Reverend Jesse Jackson, of the National Rainbow Coalition, to President William J. Clinton, March 21, 1994, Clinton Presidential Library Archives, Domestic Policy Council, Bruce Reed, Crime [OA 101824], box 77, folder 2.
27. Michelle Alexander, *The New Jim Crow: Mass Incarceration in the Age of Colorblindness* (New York: New Press, 2010), 13.
28. Kennedy, *Persistence of the Color Line*, 19.
29. Kathleen M. Blee, "Racial Violence in the United States," *Ethnic and Racial Studies* 28, no. 4 (July 2005): 613–614.
30. Slavoj Žižek, *Violence* (New York: Picador, 2008), 1.
31. Kenji Yoshino, *Covering: The Hidden Assault on Our Civil Rights* (New York: Random House, 2006), 26.
32. Maggie Nelson, *The Art of Cruelty: A Reckoning* (New York: Norton, 2011), 40.

CHAPTER 2   THE INVENTION OF HATE CRIMES

1. For scholarship on the lived experience of bias-motivated victimization, see Benjamin Bowling, *Violent Racism, Victimization, Policing and Social Context* (Oxford: Clarendon, 1998); Gregory M. Herek, Jeannine C. Cogan, and J. Roy Gillis, "Victims Experiences in Hate Crimes Based on Sexual Orientation," *Journal of Social Issues* 58, no. 2 (2002): 319–339; Frank van Germert, "Chicken Kills Hawk: Gay Murders during the Eighties in Amsterdam," *Journal of Homosexuality* 26, no. 4 (1994): 149–174; Edward Dunbar, "Race, Gender, and Sexual Orientation in Hate Crime Victimization: Identity Politics or Identity Risk?," *Violence and Victims* 21, no. 3 (June 2006): 323–337; Kevin T. Berrill and Gregory M. Herek, "Primary and Secondary Victimization in Anti-Gay Hate Crimes," *Journal of Interpersonal Violence* 5, no. 3 (September 1990): 401–413; Edward Dunbar, "Hate Crime Patterns in Los Angeles County: Demographic and Behavioral Factors of Victim Impact and Reporting of

Crime" (paper, congressional briefing cosponsored by the American Psychological Association and the Society for Psychological Study of Social Issues, Washington, DC, November 1997). As the titles in this note suggest, research on the psychological, financial, emotional effects of bias-motivated victimization is skewed toward victims of anti-gay hate crimes.

2. Sergeant-Detective William Johnston, letter to Superintendent Joseph C. Carter, "1990 Yearly Report," January 1991, Boston Public Library, Government Documents Department.

3. Francis M. Roache, police commissioner, "Letter to Mayor of the City of Boston Raymond L. Flynn" with attached "Report on Civil Rights Investigations Conducted by the Boston Police Department—Community Disorders Unit," February 2, 1987, Northeastern University Archive, Boston, M91, box 5, F40.

4. Judith D. Feins, Rachel G. Bratt, and Robert Hollister, "Final Report of a Study of Racial Discrimination in the Boston Housing Market" (submitted to Patterson Riley, director of the Mayor's Office of Fair Housing, November 1981), Boston Public Library, Government Documents Department, M3/B16 FH 81; Chuck Wexler, director, Police Executive Research Forum, interview by Clara S. Lewis, Washington, DC, 2008.

5. Wexler, interview.

6. Johnston, letter to Carter, "1990 Yearly Report"; see also William M. Holms, "Hate Crimes Reporting: Obstacles, Facilitators, and Strategies Executive Summary," November 17, 1992, Boston Public Library, Government Documents Department, M3 CJ 92/3 ex sum; William M. Holms, "Guidelines for Campus Police: Hate Crime Training," November 17, 1992, Boston Public Library, Government Documents Department, M3 CJ 92/2; Executive Office of Public Safety, Criminal Systems Board, Department of Public Safety, Crime Reporting Unit, "Hate Crime/ Hate Incidents in Massachusetts 1991 Annual Report," July 21, 1992, Boston Public Library, Government Documents Department, M3 CHS S5 1991.

7. Roache, "Letter to Mayor" with attached "Report on Civil Rights Investigations"; Executive Office of Public Safety, Criminal Systems Board, Department of Public Safety, Crime Reporting Unit, "Hate Crime in Massachusetts Preliminary Annual Report, January–December, 1990," April 26, 1991, Boston Public Library, Government Documents Department, M3 CHS S5.

8. Roache, "Letter to Mayor" with attached "Report on Civil Rights Investigations."

9. Wexler, interview.

10. To learn more about the ADL, visit their website at http://www.adl.org.

11. "The ADL Anti-Paramilitary Training Statute: A Response to Domestic Terrorism," in *ADL Law Report* (New York: William and Naomi Gorowitz Institute on Terrorism and Extremism, Anti-Defamation League, 1995); "Legislation: 1981, 'Model' Paramilitary Training Statute," *ADL Law Report* 8, no. 1 (Winter 1982).

12. Jeffrey P. Sinesky and David M. Raim, "ADL 'Model' Religious Vandalism Statute," Memorandum, December 1981.

13. Michael Lieberman, Anti-Defamation League Washington counsel and director of Civil Rights Policy Planning Center, interview by Clara S. Lewis, Washington, DC, March 19, 2008.

14. Ibid.

15. Sinesky and Raim, "ADL 'Model' Religious Vandalism Statute."

16. Ibid.

17. Steve M. Freeman, *Civil Rights Division Policy Background Report* (New York: Anti-Defamation League of B'nai B'rith, 1990).

18. *Racially Motivated Violence: Hearings Before the Senate Subcommittee on Criminal Justice*, HR 3914, series 1444 (July 12, 1988): 19 (statement of John Weiss, National Institute Against Prejudice and Violence).

19. *Racially Motivated Violence.*

20. *Racially Motivated Violence,* 14 (statement of Reverend C. T. Vivian, Center for Democratic Renewal).

21. *Racially Motivated Violence,* 71 (statement of Eugene S. Mornell, executive director of the L.A. County Commission on Human Rights).

22. *Hate Crime Statistics Act of 1988, Hearings Before the Subcommittee on the Constitution of the Committee on the Judiciary, United States Senate,* 100th Cong., 2nd Sess., J-100-79 (June 21, 1988): 73 (statement of John Weiss, National Institute Against Prejudice and Violence).

23. For scholarship on hate crime perpetrators, see Donald P. Green, "Causes of Hate: Economic versus Demographics" (paper, congressional briefing cosponsored by the American Psychological Association and the Society for Psychological Study of Social Issues, Washington, DC, November 1997); Donald P. Green, Jack Glaser, and Andrew Rich, "From Lynching to Gay-Bashing: The Elusive Connection between Economic Conditions and Hate Crime," *Journal of Personality and Social Psychology* 75, no. 1 (July 1998): 82–92. See also Donald P. Green, Robert P. Abelson, and Margaret Garnett, "The Distinctive Political Views of Hate-Crime Perpetrators and White Supremacists," in *Cultural Divides: Understanding and Overcoming Group Conflict,* ed. Deborah A. Prentice and Dale T. Miller (New York: Russell Sage Foundation, 1999), 429–464. For studies on the defended communities perspective, see Christopher J. Lyons, "Defending Turf: Racial Demographics and Hate Crime," *Social Forces* 87, no. 1 (September 2008): 357–385; Donald P. Green, D. Strolovitch, and J. Wong, "Defended Neighborhoods, Integration, and Racially Motivated Crime," *American Journal of Sociology* 104, no. 2 (1998): 372–403; David Jacobs and Katherine Woods, "Interracial Conflict and Interracial Homicide: Do Political and Economic Rivalries Explain White Killings of Blacks or Black Killings of Whites?," *American Journal of Sociology* 105, no. 1 (1999): 157–190; Christopher J. Lyons, "Community (Dis)organization and Racially Motivated Crime," *American Journal of Sociology* 113, no. 3 (2007): 815–863; Lauren M. McLaren, "Explaining Right-Wing Violence in Germany: A Time Series Analysis," *Social Science Quarterly* 80, no. 1 (1999): 166–180; Jeffrey D. Morenoff, Stephen W. Raudenbush, and Robert J. Sampson, "Neighborhood Inequality, Collective Efficacy and the Spatial Dynamics of Urban Violence," *Criminology* 39, no. 3 (2001): 517–560.

24. *Race Relations and Adolescents: Coping with New Realities, Hearings Before the Select Committee on Children, Youth, and Families, House of Representatives,* 100th Cong., 1st Sess. (March 27, 1987): 38 (statement of James Comer).

25. *Hate Crime Statistics Act of 1988, Hearings* (statement of William Yoshino, Midwestern regional director, Japanese American Citizens League).

26. *Ethnically Motivated Violence Against Arab-Americans, Hearings Before the Subcommittee on Criminal Justice of the Committee on the Judiciary, House of Representatives,* 99th Cong., 2nd Sess., 34 (July 16, 1986) (statement of James Abourezk, chairman, Arab-American Anti-Discrimination Committee).

27. *Anti-Gay Violence, Hearings Before the Subcommittee on Criminal Justice of the Committee on the Judiciary, House of Representatives,* 99th Cong., 2nd Sess., 132 (October 9, 1986): 5 (statement of Diana Christensen, director of the Community United Against Violence in San Francisco).

28. *Race Relations and Adolescents* (statement of George Miller).

29. *Racially Motivated Violence,* 16 (statement of Reverend C. T. Vivian).

30. *Racially Motivated Violence,* 54 (statement of Reverend Benjamin Hooks, CEO/executive director, NAACP, MD).

31. *Anti-Gay Violence,* 13 (statement of Gregory M. Herek, on behalf of the American Psychological Association).

32. *Racially Motivated Violence*, 114 (statement of John Conyers Jr.).
33. *Hate Crime Statistics Act of 1988, Hearings*, 34 (statement of James G. Abourezk, former senator).
34. Ibid., 81.
35. *Race Relations and Adolescents*, 40 (statement of James Comer).
36. *Anti-Gay Violence*, 4 (statement of Kevin Berrill).
37. *Ethnically Motivated Violence Against Arab-Americans*, 2 (statement of Nick Joe Rahall, D, WV).
38. *Racially Motivated Violence*, 27 (statement of Ronald L. Kuby, cooperating attorney, Center for Constitutional Rights, New York).
39. *Race Relations and Adolescents*, 4 (statement of Gary Orfield).
40. *Race Relations and Adolescents*, 40 (statement of James Comer).
41. *Anti-Gay Violence*, 11 (statement of David Wertheimer, executive director of the New York City Gay and Lesbian Anti-Violence Project).
42. Rick Beltz, "Divided Council Approves Penalties for Racist Attacks," *Baltimore Sun*, January 11, 1984.
43. Lena Williams, "Lack of Figures on Racial Strife Fueling Dispute," *New York Times*, April 5, 1987, 1, 20.
44. Todd S. Purdum, "The Region," *New York Times*, November 1, 1987, sec. 4, p. 6.
45. Todd S. Purdum, "Acts Linked to Increase in Bias Cases," *New York Times*, December 25, 1987, B1; See also Colman McCarthy, "Mayor Flynn and Friend," *Washington Post*, July 14, 1984, A19; Scott Bronstein, "Laws to Curb Bias Attacks Weighed," *New York Times*, March 2, 1987.
46. Colman McCarthy, "Mayor Flynn and Friend," *Washington Post*, July 14, 1984, A19.
47. "The Nation No 'Hate Crime' Listing," *Los Angeles Times*, March 22, 1985.
48. Jan Wong, "Asian Bashing: Bias Against Orientals Increases with Rivalry of Nation's Economies and Immigration of the Industrious Poor," *Wall Street Journal*, November 28, 1986.
49. Clare Anesberry, "Apparent Rise in 'Hate' Crimes Prompts Tougher State Laws, National Parley," *Wall Street Journal*, September 15, 1986.
50. Jerry Gray, "Bias Crime Up 18 Percent; and Juveniles Led the Way," *New York Times*, April 4, 1992.
51. Victoria Irwin, "Race Tensions Surface in New York," *Christian Science Monitor*, December 23, 1986.
52. Ibid., 3.
53. *Anti-Gay Violence*, 3 (statement of Kevin Berrill).
54. *Racially Motivated Violence*.
55. *Ethnically Motivated Violence Against Arab-Americans*.
56. Stephen Steinberg, *Turning Back: The Retreat from Racial Justice in American Thought and Policy* (Boston: Beacon, 1995).
57. Michael Omi and Howard Winant, *Racial Formation in the United States: From the 1960s to the 1990s*, 2nd ed. (New York: Routledge, 1994), 141.
58. Robert Reiner, *Law and Order: An Honest Citizen's Guide to Crime and Control* (Cambridge: Polity, 2007), vii.
59. Ibid, vii.
60. Ibid.
61. David Garland, *The Culture of Control: Crime and Social Order in Contemporary Society* (Chicago: University of Chicago Press, 2001); Frank Furedi, *Culture of Fear: Risk Taking and the Morality of Low Expectation*, rev. ed. (London: Continuum, 2002); Reiner, *Law and Order*.
62. David L. Altheide, "The News Media, the Problem Frame, and the Production of Fear," *Sociological Quarterly* 38, no. 4 (Autumn 1997): 663–664.

63. Martin Innes, "Signal Crimes: Detective Work, Mass Media and Constructing Collective Memory," in *Criminal Visions: Media Representations of Crime and Justice*, ed. Paul Mason (Portland, OR: Willan, 2003), 159.

64. Garland, *Culture of Control*, 11.

65. A. E. Bottoms, "Neglected Features of the Contemporary Penal System," in *The Power to Punish*, ed. David Garland and Peter Young (London: Heinemann, 1983), quoted in Sandra Walkalate, *Imagining the Victim of Crime* (Maidenhead, UK: McGraw-Hill, 2007), 20.

66. David M. Raim, former Anti-Defamation League attorney, interview by Clara S. Lewis, Washington, DC, April 9, 2008.

67. Frederick M. Lawrence, interview by Clara S. Lewis, Washington, DC, 2008.

CHAPTER 3 THE NATION AND POST-
DIFFERENCE POLITICS

1. Vice President Al Gore, second Bush-Gore debate, Wake Forest University, Winston-Salem, NC, October 11, 2000; President William J. Clinton, State of the Union Address, January 27, 2000; President Obama, "Remarks on the Enactment of the Matthew Shepard and James Byrd, Jr. Hate Crime Prevention Act," October 28, 2009, John T. Woolley and Gerhard Papers, American Presidency Project, http://www.presidency.ucsb.edu/ws/?pid=86813.

2. Pierre Bourdieu, *The Logic of Practice* (Stanford: Stanford University Press, 1990).

3. Colin Flint, *Spaces of Hate: Geographies of Discrimination and Intolerance in the United States of America* (London: Routledge, 2004), 3.

4. Rini Sumartojo, "Contesting Place: Anti-Gay and Lesbian Hate Crime in Columbus, Ohio," in *Spaces of Hate: Geographies of Discrimination and Intolerance in the United States of America*, ed. Colin Flint (London: Routledge, 2004), 87.

5. For scholarship on new or color-blind racism, see Ashley W. Doane and Eduardo Bonilla-Silva, eds., *White Out: The Continuing Significance of Racism* (New York: Routledge, 2003); David Theo Goldberg, *Racist Culture: Philosophy and the Politics of Meaning* (Cambridge, MA: Harvard University Press, 1993); Paul Gilroy, "The End of Antiracism," in *Race Critical Theories*, ed. Philomena Essed and David Theo Goldberg (Cambridge, MA: Blackwell, 2002), 249–64; David Wellman, *Portraits of White Racism*, 2nd ed. (New York: Cambridge University Press, 1993); Michael Brown, *Whitewashing Race: The Myth of a Color-Blind Society* (Berkeley: University of California Press, 2003); Tyrone Forman and Amanda Lewis, "Racial Apathy and Hurricane Katrina: The Social Anatomy of Prejudice in the Post-Civil Rights Era," *Du Bois Review* 3, no. 1 (2006): 196; Steven A. Tuch and Jack K. Martin, eds., *Racial Attitudes in the 1990s: Continuity and Change* (London: Praeger, 1997); Charles A. Gallagher, "'The End of Racism' as the New Doxa," in *White Logic, White Methods: Racism and Methodology*, ed. Tukufu Zuberi and Eduardo Bonilla-Silva (London: Rowman & Littlefield, 2008), 162–78; Eduardo Bonilla-Silva, Amanda Lewis, and David G. Embrick, "'I Did Not Get That Job Because of a Black Man . . .': The Story Lines and Testimonies of Color-Blind Racism," *Sociological Forum* 19, no. 4 (December 2004): 555; Joe R. Fagin, *Racist America* (New York: Routledge, 2000); Maria Krysan and Amanda Lewis, eds., *The Changing Terrain of Race and Ethnicity* (New York: Russell Sage Foundation, 2004); Howard Schuman, Charlotte Steeh, Lawrence Bobo, and Maria Krysan, *Racial Attitudes in America: Trend and Interpretations*, 2nd ed. (Cambridge, MA: Harvard University Press, 1997); Stephen Steinberg, *Turning Back: The Retreat from Racial Justice in American Thought and Policy* (Boston: Beacon, 1995); Lewis Killian, "Race Relations and the Nineties," *Social Forces* 69, no. 1 (1990): 1–13.

6. Tyrone A. Forman, "Color-Blind Racism and Racial Indifference: The Role of Racial Apathy in Facilitating Enduring Inequalities," in Krysan and Lewis, *Changing Terrain of Race and Ethnicity*, 59.

7. Jim Cummins, "In Jasper, Texas, Trial Begins for Three Men Accused of Dragging Black Man to His Death," *NBC News at Sunrise*, February 16, 1999.

8. John Robert, "Second Suspect Goes on Trial for the Murder of a Black Man Dragged to Death Behind a Pickup Truck in Texas," *CBS Evening News*, August 31, 1999.

9. Dan Rather, "John William King Goes on Trial for Brutal Killing of Black Man in Texas Last June," *CBS Evening News*, February 16, 1999.

10. Tom Brokaw, "Death of Victim of Wyoming Hate Crime Increases Charges Against Suspects," *NBC Nightly News*, October 12, 1998.

11. Mika Brzenski, "Mother of Murdered Gay Wyoming College Student Pushing for Hate-Crime Legislation," *CBS Morning News*, March 24, 1999.

12. Dan Rather, "University of Wyoming Student Matthew Shepard Dies from His Injuries, His Alleged Attackers Will Face Murder Charges and Many Are Calling for National Hate-Crime Legislation," *CBS Evening News*, October 12, 1998; Dan Rather, "Funeral Set for Texas Man Killed in Hate Crime," *CBS Evening News*, June 11, 1998.

13. Daniel Pedersen, "A Quiet Man's Tragic Rendezvous with Hate," *Newsweek*, March 15, 1999.

14. *Hate Crimes Prevention Act of 1998, Hearings Before the Committee on the Judiciary, United States Senate*, 105th Cong., S.J. Res 1529, J-105-115 (July 8, 1998) (statement of Reverend Charles Bergstrom).

15. *Jena 6 and the Role of Federal Intervention in Hate Crimes and Race-Related Violence in Public Schools, Hearing of the House Judiciary Committee* (October 16, 2007) (statement of John Conyers).

16. *Bias Crimes, Hearing Before the Subcommittee on Crime and Criminal Justice, Committee on the Judiciary, House of Representatives*, 102nd Cong., 2nd Sess., H521-29 (May 11, 1992) (statement of Charles E. Schumer).

17. President Bush, "Remarks on Signing the Hate Crime Statistic Act," April 23, 1990, John T. Woolley and Gerhard Papers, American Presidency Project, http://www.presidency.ucsb.edu/ws/?pid=18394.

18. *Hate Crimes Violence, Hearings Before the House of Representatives Committee on the Judiciary*, H521-101 (August 4, 1999) (statement of John Conyers).

19. Sherrilyn A. Ifill, *On the Courthouse Lawn: Confronting the Legacy of Lynching in the 21st Century* (Boston: Beacon, 2007).

20. President Obama, "Remarks on the Enactment."

21. *Hate Crimes Prevention Act of 1998* (statement of Orin Hatch).

22. *Hate Crimes Violence* (statement of Henry J. Hyde).

23. Ibid.

24. Ibid.

25. *Bias Crimes* (statement of Charles E. Schumer). During a number of speeches on the topic of hate crime, Clinton made similar connections between the nation's ability to realize its "true promise" in a global economy and working against hate crimes. See President Clinton, "Remarks on the Proposed Hate Crime Prevention Act," April 6, 1999, John T. Woolley and Gerhard Papers, American Presidency Project, http://www.presidency.ucsb.edu/ws/?pid=57365.

26. President Clinton, "Remarks on the Proposed Hate Crimes Prevention Act."

27. President Clinton, "Radio Address to the Nation," June 7, 1997, John T. Woolley and Gerhard Papers, American Presidency Project, http://www.presidency.ucsb.edu/ws/?pid=54237.

28. James B. Jacobs and Kimberly Potter, *Hate Crimes: Criminal Law and Identity Politics* (New York: Oxford University Press, 1998).

29. Bob Schieffer, "New Jersey Public Schools Combat Bias Incidents with Tolerance Education," *CBS Evening News*, January 23, 1993. The previous day, Jacqueline Adams made a parallel statement. In reporting on a hate crime that occurred at Rider College, Adams stated, "The incident here at Rider is just another outbreak of the epidemic of racism that seems to be sweeping through the nation's young people. Here in New Jersey alone, the attorney general's office reports that bias crimes were up 50 percent last year." Dan Rather (anchor) and Jacqueline Adams (byline), "Ruder College Fraternity Exhibits Blatant Racism," *CBS Evening News*, January 22, 1993.

30. *Hate Crimes Sentencing Enhancement Act of 1992, Hearing Before the Subcommittee on Crime and Criminal Justice of the Committee on the Judiciary House of Representatives*, 102 Cong., H.R. 4797, 64 (July 29, 1992).

31. "Survey Finds Decrease in Anti-Gay Violence," *New York Times*, March 9, 1994.

32. Connie Chung, "The Demonstrators," *ABC News*, December 10, 1998.

33. "An 'Epidemic of Terror,'" *New York Times*, March 24, 1996.

34. David Leavitt, "The Hate Epidemic," *New York Times*, October 18, 1998.

35. Anne Barnard, "Assault on Latinos Spur Inquiry," *New York Times*, January 13, 2009.

36. Richard Schlesinger, "Part II—On Hate Street: Gay Protest Hate Crimes in Boston," *48 Hours*, February 26, 1992.

37. *Hate Crime Statistics Act of 1988, Hearings Before the Subcommittee on the Constitution of the Committee on the Judiciary, United States Senate*, 100th Cong., 2nd Sess., J-100-79 (June 21, 1988).

38. President Clinton, "Remarks on the Legislative Agenda on Hate Crimes," September 13, 2000, John T. Woolley and Gerhard Papers, American Presidency Project, http://www.presidency.ucsb.edu/ws/?pid=1350.

39. Tom Brokaw, "Web of Hate: Hate Sites on the Web Affect Everyone," *Dateline*, July 28, 2000.

40. Michael Brick, "Three Sentences in Death of Gay Man," *New York Times*, November 21, 2007.

41. Clifford D. May, "Panel Hearings Will Examine 'Hate Crimes,'" *New York Times*, January 18, 1988.

42. President Clinton, "Remarks on the Legislative Agenda." See also President Clinton, "Remarks on the Proposed Hate Crime Legislation."

43. Chung, "The Demonstrators."

44. "An Epidemic of Terror."

45. American Psychological Association, "Hate Crime Today: An Age Old Foe in Modern Dress" (position paper, 1998). See also G. M. Herek and R. J. Gillis, "The Impact of Hate Crime Victimization" (paper, congressional briefing cosponsored by the American Psychological Association and the Society for the Psychological Study of Social Issues, Washington, DC, November 1998).

46. *Bias Crimes* (statement of Michael Riff).

47. Thalia Assuras, "White House Republicans at Odds over Proposed Hate Crime Legislation," *CBS Evening News*, October 30, 1999. For a similar remark, see President Clinton, "Letter to the Speaker of the House of Representatives on the Proposed 'Hate Crimes Prevention Act,'" July 12, 2000, John T. Woolley and Gerhard Papers, American Presidency Project, http://www.presidency.ucsb.edu/ws/?pid=1598.

48. Forman, "Color-Blind Racism and Racial Indifference," 52–53; Paul Wachtel, *Race in the Mind of America: Breaking the Vicious Circle between Blacks and Whites* (New York: Routledge, 1999), 35–36.

49. Forman, "Color-Blind Racism and Racial Indifference," 52–53.

50. Ashley W. Doane, "Rethinking Whiteness Studies," in Doane and Bonilla-Silva, *White Out*, 13.

51. Ibid., 13.

52. Forman, "Color-Blind Racism and Racial Indifference," 52–53.

53. Joachim J. Savelsberg and Ryan D. King, "Institutional Collective Memory of Hate: Law and Law Enforcement in Germany and the United States," *American Journal of Sociology* 111, no. 2 (September 2005): 611.

54. Ifill, *On the Courthouse Lawn*, 158.

55. Ibid., 155.

56. Martha Minow, *Breaking the Cycle of Hatred: Memory, Law, Repair* (Princeton, NJ: Princeton University Press, 2002), 46.

57. Frederick M. Lawrence, dean of the George Washington University Law School, interview by Clara S. Lewis, Washington, DC, April 28, 2008.

58. Donald P. Haider-Markel, "The Politics of Social Regulatory Policy: State and Federal Hate Crimes Policy and Implementation Effort," *Political Research Quarterly* 51, no. 1 (March 1998): 69, 71.

59. Jeannine Bell, *Policing Hatred: Law Enforcement, Civil Rights, and Hate Crime* (New York: New York University Press, 2002).

60. Tim Alan Garrison, *The Legal Ideology of Removal: The Southern Judiciary and the Sovereignty of Native American Nations* (Athens: University of Georgia Press, 2009); Douglas A. Blackmon, *Slavery by Another Name: The Re-enslavement of Black Americans from the Civil War to World War II* (New York: Anchor Books, 2008); Mae M. Ngai, *Impossible Subjects: Illegal Aliens and the Making of Modern America* (Princeton, NJ: Princeton University Press, 2004).

CHAPTER 4   CULTURAL CRIMINALIZATION AND
              THE FIGURE OF THE HATER

1. Kai Erikson, *Wayward Puritans* (New York: Macmillan, 1966).

2. H. L. Mencken, "Eastern Shore Kultur," *Evening Sun*, December 17, 1931, cited in Sherrilyn A. Ifill, *On the Courthouse Lawn: Confronting the Legacy of Lynching in the 21st Century* (Boston: Beacon, 2007), 63.

3. See, respectively, Susan F. Rasky, "Bush Is Sent Bill Requiring Data on Bias Crimes," *New York Times*, April 5, 1990; Todd S. Purdum, "To Counter Bias Attacks, Dinkins Is Spreading Message of Tolerance," *New York Times*, January 17, 1992; "Chicago in Shock over Latest Hate Crime," *ABC World News Tonight*, March 26, 1997; Milo Geyelin, "Color of Hate: As a Tense Trial Begins, Tampa, Fla., Confronts Costs of Racial Strife—Whites Accused of Torching Black Tourist; City Fears Effect on Its Economy—'Mean' Suspects, Shaky Case," *Wall Street Journal*, August 24, 1993; Tom Brokaw, "Death of Victim of Wyoming Hate Crime Increases Charges Against Suspects," *NBC Nightly News*, October 12, 1998; "Second Suspect Goes on Trial for the Murder of a Black Man Dragged to Death Behind a Pickup Truck in Texas," *CBS Evening News*, August 31, 1999; Richard Turner, "All Carnage, All the Time," *Newsweek*, August 13, 1999. LexisNexis Academic (October 23, 2009).

4. "Bias Crimes on Increase; Pre-Trial Hearing in Florida Is Example," *CBS Morning News*, May 6, 1993. See also "Two Men Found Guilty of Setting Tourists on Fire Could Face Life in Prison," *CBS Morning News*, September 8, 1993.

5. Geyelin, "Color of Hate."

6. Ted Koppel, "A Matter of Choice? Gays, Straights, and the Search for Common Grounds; Roanoke Newspaper Profiles Local Gays and Lesbians Causing Controversy," *Nightline*, May 21, 2002.

7. Lisa Salters, "Mourners Gather for Matthew Shepard," *ABC Good Morning America*, October 13, 1998.

8. Brokaw, "Death of Victim." For similar descriptions of Henderson and McKinney, see James Brooke, "Men Held in Beating Lived on the Fringes," *New York Times*, October 16, 1998.

9. Bob Arnot, "Memories of Matthew; Parents of Murdered College Student, Matthew Shepard, Speak about Their Son," *Dateline*, February 5, 1999.

10. Geyelin, "Color of Hate."

11. Forrest Sawyer, "Damage Assessment of Ames Scandal," *ABC World News Tonight*, December 8, 1995; Forrest Sawyer, "Soldiers Involved in Hate Crime," *ABC World News Tonight*, December 8, 1995.

12. Ian Urbina, "Victim Tells Police of Possible Motive for Abduction," *New York Times*, September 20, 2007. See also Ian Urbina, "Woman Recants Story of West Virginia Trailer," *New York Times*, October 22, 2009.

13. Brokaw, "Death of Victim." For similar descriptions of Henderson and McKinney, see Brooke, "Men Held in Beating."

14. Geyelin, "Color of Hate."

15. Rick Bragg, "Unfathomable Crime, Unlikely Figure," *New York Times*, June 17, 1998.

16. "Wen Ho Lee Case Raises Unsettling Questions for Asian-Americans," *CNN*, September 13, 2000.

17. Alex Chadwick, "Japanese-Americans Target of Violence," *Morning Edition*, National Public Radio, February 27, 1992.

18. Christine Choy and Renee Tajima-Pena, *Who Killed Vincent Chin?* (documentary film, 1989).

19. "Stiff and Proper," *New York Times*, April 6, 1999.

20. Michael Janofsky, "Parents of Gay Obtain Mercy for His Killer," *New York Times*, November 5, 1999.

21. Andrew Murr and Howard Fineman, "Echoes of a Murder in Wyoming," *Newsweek*, October 26, 1998.

22. Brooke, "Men Held in Beating."

23. Soledad O'Brien, "Citizens of Laramie, Wyoming, Show Disdain for Hate in Their Community," *NBC Nightly News*, October 10, 1998.

24. Martin Innes, "Signal Crimes: Detective Work, Mass Media and Constructing Collective Memory," in *Criminal Visions: Media Representations of Crime and Justice*, ed. Paul Mason (Portland, OR: Willan, 2003), 159.

25. Brooke, "Men Held in Beating."

26. Joshua Hammer, "The 'Gay Panic' Defense," *Newsweek*, November 8, 1999.

27. Arnot, "Memories of Matthew."

28. Brokaw, "Death of Victim." For similar descriptions of Henderson and McKinney see Brooke, "Men Held in Beating."

29. *ABC News*, November 26, 2004.

30. Sawyer, "Soldiers Involved in Hate Crime"; Eric Schmitt, "Inquiry by Army Focuses on Hate," *New York Times*, December 13, 1995.

31. Edmund L. Andrews, "Slaying Lead Army to Look at Extremism," *New York Times*, December 10, 1995.

32. "The Enemy Within: Racists in the Ranks," *48 Hours*, June 26, 1997.

33. For stories that conflate the hate crime and hate group problem, see Linda Vester, "Los Angeles Police Department Trying to Prevent Spread of Racial Violence with Help of New Computer Database," *NBC News at Sunrise*, August 16, 1999; Dan Rather, "Changing Face of Hate Crimes from Groups Committing Them to Individuals," *CBS Evening News*, August 11, 1999; Julie Chen, "Civil Rights Leaders Expanding Push for Tougher Federal Hate Crime Laws," *CBS This Morning*, July 13, 1999; Carla Wohl and Terry Moran, "Trying to Stop Hate Crimes," *ABC World*

News This Morning, April 7, 1999; Jack Ford, "The Occurrence of Hate Crimes Today," *Sunday Today*, February 28, 1999; "Mark McEwen and Morris Dees Discuss the Murder of James Byrd and the Hate Crimes Aspect of Murder," *CBS This Morning*, June 11, 1998; Kevin Sack, "Hate Groups in United States Are Growing, Report Says," *New York Times*, March 3, 1998; Roland Smothers, "Hate Groups Seen Growing as Neo-Nazis Draw Young," *New York Times*, February 19, 1992.

34. Brian Williams, "In Depth; Hate Crimes on rise in US," *NBC Nightly News*, June 10, 2009.

35. Charles Gibson, "A Closer Look; Hate Crimes," *World News with Charles Gibson*, May 2, 2007.

36. Bob Herbert, "In America; Staring at Hatred," *New York Times*, February 28, 1999.

37. As part of Jasper's racial reconciliation process following Byrd's murder, the town removed the fence segregating the cemetery.

38. Rick Lyman, "A Guilty Verdict in Texas Dragging Death," *New York Times*, February 28, 1999.

39. Dan Rather, "Ongoing Trial in Jasper, Texas, of a Man Accused of Dragging a Black Man to His Death," *CBS Evening News*, February 19, 1999; Dan Rather, "John William King Sentenced to Death by Lethal Injection for the Dragging Death of James Byrd Jr.," *CBS Evening News*, February 25, 1999. The same quotation was aired again on *CBS This Morning*; see Jane Robelot, "Texas Jury Sentences John William King to Death for the Murder of James Byrd," *CBS This Morning*, February 26, 1999.

40. Ann Curry, "Day Two of Testimony in Murder Trial of John William King," *Today*, February 17, 1999.

41. Rather, "John William King Sentenced to Death."

42. Jim Axelrod, "Counseling Children on Racism," *CBS Evening News*, February 25, 1999.

43. Innes, "Signal Crimes," 159.

44. Ann Curry, "Recap of NBC's Today Show's News, 7:30 AM," *Today*, February 16, 1999.

45. Dawn Fratangelo, "People of Jasper, Texas, Prepare for Trial over the Murder of James Byrd Jr.," *NBC Nightly News*, January 24, 1999.

46. Dan Rather, "John William King Goes on Trial for Brutal Killing of Black Man in Texas Last June," *CBS Evening News*, February 16, 1999.

47. Jane Robelot, "Opening Statements to Begin in racially Charged Trial in Jasper, Texas," *CBS This Moring*, February 16, 1999.

48. Peter Jennings, "Jury in Jasper, TX Sees Grisly Evidence," *ABC World News Tonight*, February 17, 1999.

49. Bragg, "Unfathomable Crime, Unlikely Figure."

50. Tom Brokaw, "John William King Became a Racist in Prison," *NBC Nightly News*, February 23, 1999.

51. Charles Gibson, "Byrd Murder Trial Death Sentence," *ABC Good Morning America*, February 26, 1999.

52. See, respectively, John Carlson, "Furrow Belonged in a Hospital, Not on the Street," *Wall Street Journal*, August 18, 1999; Antonio Mora, "Pittsburgh Funeral," *ABC Good Morning America*, May 1, 2000; Katie Couric, "Morris Dees, SPLC, Discusses Last Week's Church Massacre in Texas," *Today*, September 20, 1999.

53. For coverage of Buford Furrow's case, see World-Wide. *Wall Street Journal*, January 25, 2001; World-Wide, *Wall Street Journal*, August 31, 1999; World-Wide, *Wall Street Journal*, August 20, 1999; "Reinventing Probation," *Wall Street Journal*, August 19, 1999; Carlson, "Furrow Belonged in a Hospital"; World-Wide, *Wall Street Journal*, August 13, 1999; Andrew Sullivan, "What's So Bad about Hate," *New York Times*,

September 26, 1999; "Gun Control Gains in California," *New York Times*, August 28, 1999; Alvin F. Poussaint, "They Hate. They Kill. Are They Insane?," *New York Times*, August 26, 1999; James Sterngold, "United States Indicts Supremacist in Mailman's Killing," *New York Times*, August 20, 1999; "National New Briefs; Neo-Nazis Cancel March Over Los Angeles Attack," *New York Times*, August 19, 1999; Bob Herbert, "In America; America's Twin Evils," *New York Times*, August 15, 1999; "The Hateful Agenda of Ignorance," *New York Times*, August 15, 1999; Timothy Egan, "Racist Shootings Test Limits of Health System, and Laws," *New York Times*, August 14, 1999; "A Crime of Hate?," *20/20*, August 11, 1999; "Racism as a Mental Illness," *Nightline*, May 31, 2001; "Brian Levin, Professor at Cal State University Discusses Hate Crimes and Hate Groups," *NBC News*, August 12, 1999; Dan Rather, "Wake Up Call; Washington State Officials Knew Buford Furrow Was a Dangerous Man Before He Killed and Wounded Adults and Children at the Jewish Community Center in Los Angeles," *60 Minutes*, March 27, 2001.

54. See, respectively, "Gun Control Gains in California"; Vanessa O'Connell and Paul M. Barrett, "Bill to Ban Police Gun Trade-Ins for Discounts Is Introduced in Congress," *Wall Street Journal*, November 19, 1999; "United States Indicts Supremacist in Mailman's Killing," *New York Times*, August 20, 1999.

55. Carlson, "Furrow Belonged in a Hospital."

56. See, respectively, "Brian Levin, Professor at Cal State University, Discusses Hate Crimes"; "National News Briefs; Neo-Nazis Cancel March over Los Angeles Attack," *New York Times*, August 19, 1999.

57. Rather, "Wake Up Call."

58. Turner, "All Carnage, All the Time."

59. Alison Stewart, "ABC World News Now Headlines," *World News Now*, March 27, 2001; Antonio Mora, "White Supremacist Buford Furrow Sentenced to Life in Prison," *ABC Good Morning America*, March 27, 2001; John Seigenthaler, "Buford Furrow Sentenced to Life in Prison," *Today*, March 27, 2002; Dan Rather, "Buford Furrow Sentenced to Life in Prison Today," *CBS Evening News*, March 26, 2001; Dorothy McIntyre, "ABC's World News Now Headlines," *World News Now*, January 24, 2001; Jim Sciutto, "ABC's World News This Morning Headlines," *World News This Morning*, January 24, 2001; Antonio Mora, "White Supremacist Buford Furrow to Plead Guilty of Hate Crime Chargers," *ABC Good Morning America*, January 24, 2001; Julie Chen, "White Supremacist Buford Furrow Expected to Plead Guilty to Federal Hate Crime Charges," *CBS Morning News*, January 24, 2001; Ann Curry, "Accused Shooter at Jewish Community Center to Plead Guilty," *Today*, January 24, 2001; Mark McEwen, "Child Injured in Shooting at Los Angeles Community Center Returns Home," *CBS This Morning*, September 24, 1999; Juju Chang, "Preparing for Dennis," *ABC Good Morning America*, August 30, 1999; Thalia Assuras, "Anti-Hate March Is Held in Los Angeles," *CBS This Morning*, August 23, 1999; Antonio Mora, "Bingo for Health," *ABC Good Morning America*, August 20, 1999; Aaron Brown, "Postal Worker Buried in Los Angeles," *ABC World News Saturday*, August 14, 1999; Russ Mitchell, "Funeral Services Today for Slain Mail Carrier," *Saturday Morning CBS*, August 14, 1999; Sharyl Attkisson, "Funeral Held in Whittier California, for Joseph Ileto, Killed by Buford Furrow in Shooting Rampage," *CBS Evening News*, August 14, 1999; Julie Chen, "Buford Furrow Charged with Murder and Attempted Murder, Could Face Death Penalty," *CBS Morning News*, August 13, 1999; Tony Perkins, "Salt Lake City in Tornado," *ABC Good Morning America*, August 12, 1999.

60. Andrew Murr, "A Visitor from the Dark Side," *Newsweek*, August 23, 1999.

61. Fred Francis, "LA Shooter Reportedly Racially Motivated and Used Gun That Was Supposedly Outlawed," *NBC Nightly News*, August 11, 1999.

62. Peter Jennings, "Profile of Buford Furrow Is Too Familiar," *ABC World News Tonight*, August 11, 1999.
63. Ted Koppel, "The Twisted Story of Buford O'Neal Furrow," *Nightline*, August 11, 1999.
64. Egan, "Racist Shootings Test Limits." For similar coverage, see Peter Jennings, "Massive Manhunt in California Is Over," *ABC World News Tonight*, August 11, 1999.
65. AP photo by Laura Rauch, August 11, 1999, http://www.apimages.com/metadata/Index/Jewish-Center-Shooting/aceb65e13cce4310bd0d1d38c15b3c4b/1/0.
66. Taken in Hayden Lake, Idaho, in 1995, www.adl.org/learn/ext_us/aryan_nations.asp?xp.
67. "Hateful Agenda of Ignorance."
68. Edward Dunbar, "Hate Crime Patterns in Los Angeles County: Demographic and Behavioral Factors of Victim Impact and Reporting of Crime" (paper, congressional briefing cosponsored by the American Psychological Association and the Society for Psychological Study of Social Issues, Washington, DC, November 1997).
69. See http://www.apa.org/ppo/issues/pfranklin.html.
70. John Hartigan Jr., *Odd Tribes: Towards a Cultural Analysis of White People* (Durham, NC: Duke University Press, 2005), 118–19.
71. John Hartigan Jr., "Who Are These White People? 'Rednecks,' 'Hillbillies,' and 'White Trash' as Marked Racial Subject," in *White Out: The Continuing Significance of Racism*, ed. Ashley W. Doane and Eduardo Bonilla-Silva (New York: Routledge, 2003), 111.
72. Robert Reiner, *Law and Order: An Honest Citizen's Guide to Crime and Control* (Cambridge: Polity, 2007).
73. Innes, "Signal Crimes," 159.
74. David L. Altheide, "The News Media, the Problem Frame, and the Production of Fear," *Sociological Quarterly* 38, no. 4 (Autumn 1997): 663–664.

Chapter 5   Hate Crime Victimhood and
            Post-Difference Citizenship

1. Maria Newman, "Young Bias-Attack Victim Tries to Laugh Off the Pain," *New York Times*, January 16, 1992. For a more detailed report on the crime, see Lynda Richardson, "61 Acts of Bias: One Fuse Lights Many Different Explosions," *New York Times*, January 28, 1992.
2. Basia Spalek, *Crime Victims: Theory, Policy, and Practice* (New York: Palgrave, 2006); Sandra Walklate, *Imagining the Victims of Crime* (London: Open University Press, 2007). For scholarship on the lived experience of bias-motivated victimization, particularly secondary victimization, see Benjamin Bowling, *Violent Racism, Victimization, Policing and Social Context* (Oxford: Clarendon, 1998); Gregory M. Herek, Jeannine C. Cogan, and J. Roy Gillis, "Victims Experiences in Hate Crimes Based on Sexual Orientation," *Journal of Social Issues* 58, no. 2 (2002): 319–339; Frank van Germert, "Chicken Kills Hawk: Gay Murders during the Eighties in Amsterdam," *Journal of Homosexuality* 26, no. 4 (1994): 149–174; Edward Dunbar, "Race, Gender, and Sexual Orientation in Hate Crime Victimization: Identity Politics or Identity Risk?," *Violence and Victims* 21, no. 3 (June 2006): 323–337; Kevin T. Berrill and Gregory M. Herek, "Primary and Secondary Victimization in Anti-Gay Hate Crimes," *Journal of Interpersonal Violence* 5, no. 3 (September 1990): 401–413. As the titles in this note suggest, research on the psychological, financial, emotional effects of bias-motivated victimization focuses mainly on victims of anti-gay hate crimes.

3. Erving Goffman, *Stigma: Notes on the Management of Spoiled Identity* (Englewood Cliffs: NJ: Prentice Hall, 1963).

4. Evelyn Nakano Glenn, "Constructing Citizenship: Exclusion, Subordination, and Resistance: Presidential Address," *American Sociological Review* 76, no. 1 (February 2011): 3.

5. Kenji Yoshino, *Covering: The Hidden Assault on Our Civil Rights* (New York: Random House, 2006), preface.

6. Jamil Salmi, "Violence in Democratic Societies: Towards an Analytic Framework," in *Beyond Criminology: Taking Harm Seriously*, ed. Paddy Hillyard, Christina Pantazis, Steve Tombs, and Dave Gordon (Nova Scotia: Frenwood, 2004), 59.

7. Bob Arnot, "Memories of Matthew; Parents of Murdered College Student, Matthew Shepard, Speak about Their Son," *Dateline*, February 5, 1999.

8. For more on gay rights movements in American history, see Scott Barclay, Mary Bernstein, and Anna-Maria Marchall, eds., *Queer Mobilizations: LGBT Activists Confront the Law* (New York: New York University Press, 2009); John D'Emilio, William B. Turner, and Urvashi Vaid, eds., *Creating Change: Sexuality, Public Policy, and Civil Rights* (New York: St. Martin's Press, 2000); Diane Helene Miller, *Freedom to Differ: The Shaping of Gay and Lesbian Struggle for Civil Rights* (New York: New York University Press, 1998); and Vincent J. Samar, ed., *The Gay Rights Movement* (Chicago: Fitroy Dearborn, 2001).

9. Report quoted by Kevin T. Berrill and Gregory M. Herek, "Primary and Secondary Victimization in Anti-Gay Hate Crimes," *Journal of Interpersonal Violence* 5, no. 3 (September 1990): 401, 403.

10. Much like the coverage of Matthew Shepard's case, reports on Gaither focused on his close relationship within his parents. Gaither was a caregiver, a home decorator, and a choir singer. These reports amplify Gaither's innocence by highlighting the fact that he did not flaunt his sexuality. They also essentialize gayness and reproduce stereotypes about gay men's innate kitsch sensibilities.

11. See, respectively, Diane Sawyer, "A Night of Terror," *20/20*, October 14, 1998; Michael Cooper, "Killing Shakes Complacency of the Gay Rights Movement, *New York Times*, October 21, 1998; James Brooke, "Gay Man Dies from Attack, Fanning Outrage and Debate," *New York Times*, October 13, 1998.

12. Sawyer, "Night of Terror."

13. As Roger O'Neil reported for NBC's *Saturday Today*, at the funeral, Dennis Shepard "made no mention of his son's homosexuality. . . . But, as the young boy's mother, Judy, sobbed, the father spoke not of hate, but his son's loving heart." Roger O'Neil, "Funeral Service for Matthew Shepard Held Amid Controversy," *Saturday Today*, October 17, 1998.

14. Arnot, "Memories of Matthew."

15. http://www.wiredstrategies.com/mrshep.htm (accessed June 29, 2013).

16. Arnot, "Memories of Matthew."

17. "Billy Jack Gaither's Life and Death," *New York Times*, March 9, 1999.

18. David Firestone, "Murder Reveals Double Life of Being Gay in Rural South," *New York Times*, March 16, 1999.

19. Len Cannon, "Billy Jack; Murder of Gay Alabama Man Being Ruled a Hate Crime," *Dateline*, March 10, 1999.

20. Kevin Sack, "2 Confess to Killing Man, Saying He Made a Sexual Advance," *New York Times*, March 5, 1999.

21. "Accomplice Convicted in Killing," *New York Times*, August 6, 1999.

22. John Quiñones, "Small Town Secrets," *20/20*, March 10, 1999.

23. Daniel Pedersen and Arlyn Tobias Gajilan, "A Quiet Man's Tragic Rendezvous with Hate," *Newsweek*, March 15 1999.

24. "Billy Jack Gaither's Life and Death."

25. Firestone, "Murder Reveals Double Life."

26. Dan Frosch, "Death of Transgender Women Is Called a Hate Crime," *New York Times*, August 2, 2008.

27. Beth Loffreda, *Loosing Matthew Shepard: Life and Politics in the Aftermath of Anti-Gay Murder* (New York: Columbia University Press, 2000), 140.

28. Ted Koppel, "Close to Home; Questions Raised about Race, Sex, and Hate in Grant Town, West Virginia, Because of the Murder of J. R. Warren," *Nightline*, February 8, 2001. For more coverage of Warren's case, see Bryant Gumbel, "Brenda and Arthur Warren Sr., Parents of 'J.R.' Warren, and Detective Doris James Discuss the Beating Death of Arthur Warren Jr.," *CBS Early Show*, July 12, 2000; Julie Chen, "Two Teen-Age Boys Accused of Murdering African-American Gay Man in West Virginia," *CBS Morning News*, July 11, 2000.

29. Randal C. Archibold, "Racial Hate Feeds a Gang War's Senseless Killing," *New York Times*, January 17, 2007.

30. Gwen Ifill, "Daughters of James Byrd Testifies Before Congress," *NBC Nightly News*, July 8, 1998. For examples of similar news coverage of Byrd's relatives, see Charles Gibson, "Byrd Murder Trial Death Sentence," *ABC Good Morning America*, February 26, 1999; Tom Brokaw, "Trial Begins for First Man Charged in Texas Hate Crime Murder of James Byrd," *NBC Nightly News*, February 16, 1999; Linda Vester, "FBI Investigates Murder of Black Man in Texas," *NBC News*, June 10, 1998.

31. Sharyl Attkisson, "Daughter of James Byrd Says Jasper Does Not Have Racial Problems," *CBS Morning News*, June 12, 1998.

32. Jane Robelot, "Funeral Set for Texas Man Killed in Hate Crime," *CBS This Morning*, June 11, 1998.

33. Ann Curry, "Jamie Byrd Talks about Life after Gruesome Racial Murder of Her Father, James Byrd Jr.," *NBC Nightly News*, May 18, 1999.

34. Milo Geyelin, "Color of Hate: As a Tense Trial Begins, Tampa, Fla., Confronts Costs of Racial Strife—Whites Accused of Torching Black Tourist; City Fears Effect on Its Economy—'Mean' Suspects, Shaky Case," *Wall Street Journal*, August 24, 1993.

35. Koppel, "Close to Home." For more coverage of Warren's case, see Gumbel, "Brenda and Arthur Warren Sr."; Chen, "Two Teen-Age Boys Accused."

36. Robelot, "Funeral Set for Texas Man."

37. Connie Chung, "Roy Smith's America," *20/20*, July 6, 1998.

38. For more on the Emmett Till case, see David W. Houck and Mathew A. Grindy, *Emmett Till and the Mississippi Press* (Jackson: University of Mississippi Press, 2008).

39. See Dan Rather, "US Investigators Look into Rash of Hate Crimes Against People Perceived as Middle Eastern or Followers of Islam," *CBS Evening News*, September 18, 2001.

40. Matt Lauer, "Intolerance Is Still a Problem in America," *Today*, January 27, 2003. For a similarly structured story on a Muslim family who lost their eldest son, an emergency medical technician, in the 9/11 attacks, see Dan Rather, "Double Jeopardy; Muslim Families in America Become the Target of Hate Crimes," *48 Hours*, September 21, 2001. For an example of a Muslim American advocacy group leader accepting and legitimating post-9/11 racial, ethnic, and religious profiling practices, see Dan Rather, "Acts of Violence Against Arab Americans in the Wake of Tuesday's Terrorists Attacks on the US," *CBS Evening News*, September 16, 2001.

41. John Berman, "Family of Hate Crime Victim May Be Deported Pakistani Man Killed in Texas," *ABC News*, January 15, 2003.

42. Derek McGinty and Alison Stewart, "Muslims Become Victims of Retaliatory Hate Crimes in Wake of Terrorist Attack," *World News Now*, September 27, 2001.

43. Jeffrey Zaslow, "How a Rumor Spread by Email Laid Low an Arab's Restaurant—It Said the Staff Was Jubilant on Sept. 11; Detroit Rallies Behind the Sheik, to No Avail," *Wall Street Journal*, March 13, 2002.

44. Nazia Kazi, "Islamophilia and Representations of the 'Good' American Muslim" (paper, Interrogating Diversity: Representation, Power, and Social Justice, American University, March 21, 2008).

45. Christopher J. Lyons, "Stigma or Sympathy? Attributions of Fault to Hate Crime Victims and Offenders," *Social Psychology Quarterly* 69, no. 1 (March 2006): 39.

46. Kellina M. Craig and Craig R. Waldo, "So, What's a Hate Crime Anyway? Young Adults' Perceptions of Hate Crimes, Victims and Perpetrators," *Law and Human Behavior* 20, no. 2 (April 1996): 119.

47. Spalek, *Crime Victims*, 5.

48. Walklate, *Imagining the Victims of Crime*, 22, 24.

EPILOGUE

1. Mary Coble, e-mail interview by Clara S. Lewis, December 24, 2011.

2. Michael O'Sullivan, "'Note to Self': Painful Reminders of Crimes," *Washington Post*, September 2, 2005, WE47.

3. Sontag, cited in Maggie Nelson, *The Art of Cruelty: A Reckoning* (New York: Norton, 2011), 61.

4. Grant H. Kester, *Conversation Pieces: Community and Conversation in Modern Art* (Berkeley: University of California Press, 2004), 9.

5. Ibid., 9.

6. Shannon Jackson, *Social Works: Performing Art, Supporting Publics* (London: Routledge, 2011), 247.

7. Nelson, *Art of Cruelty*, 5.

8. Kester, *Conversation Pieces*, 108.

9. Ibid., 8.

10. Ibid., 8.

11. Michael Kranish, "A Clash in Lifestyle, a Death in Bangor," *Boston Globe*, July 13, 1984.

12. Judy Harrison, "Events to Mark 1984 Slaying of Gay Man in Bangor," *Bangor Daily News*, July 8, 2009; Judy Harrison, "Where Are Charlie Howard's Killers?," *Bangor Daily News*, July 13, 2009.

13. Whitney Dow and Marco Williams, *Two Towns of Jasper* (Independent Television Service and National Black Programming Consortium, 2002).

14. Michael Omi and Howard Winant, *Racial Formation in the United States: From the 1960s to the 1990s*, 2nd ed. (New York: Routledge, 1994), 159.

15. Ta-Nehisi Coates, "A Muscular Empathy," *Atlantic*, December 14, 2011, http://www.theatlantic.com/national/archive/2011/12/a-muscular-empathy/249984/.

16. Dimitrina Petrova, "Racial Discrimination and the Rights of Minority Cultures," in *International Law, Human Rights and the United Nations*, ed. Sandra Fredman (Oxford: Oxford University Press, 2001), 49.

17. Simon Pemberton, "A Theory of Moral Indifference: Understanding the Production of Harm by Capitalist Society," in *Beyond Criminology: Taking Harm Seriously*, ed. Paddy Hillyard, Christina Pantazis, Steve Tombs, and Dave Gordon (London: Pluto Press, 2004), 71.

INDEX

About the Author

Clara S. Lewis currently teaches at Stanford University. She has published articles on hate crimes, vinyasa yoga, and mechanization at Krispy Kreme Doughnuts. She is beginning new research on the legacy of eugenics in the United States.

CPSIA information can be obtained at www.ICGtesting.com
Printed in the USA
BVOW08s1345041113

335115BV00002BA/4/P